Excel 2007: Advanced

Student Manual

Excel 2007: Advanced

Series Product Managers: Charles G. Blum and Adam A. Wilcox
Writer: Gary Young
Developmental Editors: Micky Markert and Don Tremblay
Copyeditor: Catherine Oliver
Keytester: Cliff Coryea
Series Designer: Adam A. Wilcox
Cover Designer: Abby Scholz

For more information go to www.axzopress.com.

Trademarks

ILT Series is a trademark of Axzo Press.

Microsoft is a trademark or registered trademark of Microsoft Corporation in the United States and/or other countries.

Some of the product names and company names used in this book have been used for identification purposes only and may be trademarks or registered trademarks of their respective manufacturers and sellers.

Disclaimers

We reserve the right to revise this publication and make changes from time to time in its content without notice.

Axzo Press is independent from Microsoft Corporation, and not affiliated with Microsoft in any manner. While this publication may be used in assisting individuals to prepare for a Microsoft Business Certification exam, Microsoft, its dedicated program administrator, and Axzo Press do not warrant that use of this publication will ensure passing a Microsoft Business Certification exam.

Student Manual
ISBN-10: 1-4239-1816-9
ISBN-13: 978-1-4239-1816-5

Student Manual with data CD and CBT
ISBN-10: 1-4239-1818-5
ISBN-13: 978-1-4239-1818-9

Printed in the United States of America

1 2 3 4 5 6 7 8 9 10 GLOB 13 12 11

What is the Microsoft Business Certification Program?

The Microsoft Business Certification Program enables candidates to show that they have something exceptional to offer—proven expertise in Microsoft Office programs. The two certification tracks allow candidates to choose how they want to exhibit their skills, either through validating skills within a specific Microsoft product or taking their knowledge to the next level and combining Microsoft programs to show that they can apply multiple skill sets to complete more complex office tasks. Recognized by businesses and schools around the world, over 3 million certifications have been obtained in over 100 different countries. The Microsoft Business Certification Program is the only Microsoft-approved certification program of its kind.

What is the Microsoft Certified Application Specialist Certification?

Microsoft
CERTIFIED
Application Specialist

The Microsoft Certified Application Specialist Certification exams focus on validating specific skill sets within each of the Microsoft® Office system programs. The candidate can choose which exam(s) they want to take according to which skills they want to validate. The available Application Specialist exams include:

- Using Microsoft® Windows Vista™
- Using Microsoft® Office Word 2007
- Using Microsoft® Office Excel® 2007
- Using Microsoft® Office PowerPoint® 2007
- Using Microsoft® Office Access 2007
- Using Microsoft® Office Outlook® 2007

What is the Microsoft Certified Application Professional Certification?

Microsoft
CERTIFIED
Application Professional

The Microsoft Certified Application Professional Certification exams focus on a candidate's ability to use the 2007 Microsoft® Office system to accomplish industry-agnostic functions, for example Budget Analysis and Forecasting, or Content Management and Collaboration. The available Application Professional exams currently include:

- Organizational Support
- Creating and Managing Presentations
- Content Management and Collaboration
- Budget Analysis and Forecasting

What do the Microsoft Business Certification Vendor of Approved Courseware logos represent?

Microsoft CERTIFIED Application Specialist | Approved Courseware

Microsoft CERTIFIED Application Professional | Approved Courseware

The logos validate that the courseware has been approved by the Microsoft® Business Certification Vendor program and that these courses cover objectives that will be included in the relevant exam. It also means that after utilizing this courseware, you may be prepared to pass the exams required to become a Microsoft Certified Application Specialist or Microsoft Certified Application Professional.

For more information

To learn more about the Microsoft Certified Application Specialist or Professional exams[1], visit www.microsoft.com/learning/msbc.

To learn about other Microsoft Certified Application Specialist approved courseware from Axzo Press, please visit www.axzopress.com.

[1]The availability of Microsoft Certified Application exams varies by Microsoft Office program, program version, and language. Visit www.microsoft.com/learning for exam availability.

Contents

Introduction — iii

Topic A: About the manual iv
Topic B: Setting your expectations vii
Topic C: Re-keying the course x

Advanced functions — 1-1

Topic A: Logical functions 1-2
Topic B: Math and statistical functions 1-9
Topic C: Financial functions 1-19
Topic D: Displaying and printing formulas 1-21
Unit summary: Advanced functions 1-24

Lookups and data tables — 2-1

Topic A: Using lookup functions 2-2
Topic B: Using MATCH and INDEX 2-8
Topic C: Creating data tables 2-12
Unit summary: Lookups and data tables 2-16

Advanced list management — 3-1

Topic A: Validating cell entries 3-2
Topic B: Exploring database functions 3-8
Unit summary: Advanced list management 3-12

PivotTables and PivotCharts — 4-1

Topic A: Working with PivotTables 4-2
Topic B: Rearranging PivotTables 4-7
Topic C: Formatting PivotTables 4-12
Topic D: PivotCharts 4-16
Unit summary: PivotTables and PivotCharts 4-18

Exporting and importing — 5-1

Topic A: Exporting and importing text files 5-2
Topic B: Exporting and importing XML data 5-10
Topic C: Querying external databases 5-18
Unit summary: Exporting and importing 5-25

Analytical options — 6-1

Topic A: Goal Seek and Solver 6-2
Topic B: The Analysis ToolPak 6-11
Topic C: Scenarios 6-14
Topic D: Views 6-22
Unit summary: Analytical options 6-25

Macros and custom functions — 7-1

Topic A: Running and recording a macro 7-2
Topic B: Working with VBA code 7-10
Topic C: Creating functions 7-14
Unit summary: Macros and custom functions 7-16

Conditional formatting and SmartArt **8-1**

Topic A: Conditional formatting with graphics 8-2
Topic B: SmartArt graphics 8-10
Unit summary: Conditional formatting and SmartArt 8-14

Course summary **S-1**

Topic A: Course summary S-2
Topic B: Continued learning after class S-4

Quick reference **Q-1**

Glossary **G-1**

Index **I-1**

Introduction

After reading this introduction, you will know how to:

A Use ILT Series training manuals in general.

B Use prerequisites, a target student description, course objectives, and a skills inventory to properly set your expectations for the course.

C Re-key this course after class.

Topic A: About the manual

ILT Series philosophy

ILT Series computer training manuals facilitate your learning by providing structured interaction with the software itself. While we provide text to explain difficult concepts, the hands-on activities are the focus of our courses. By paying close attention as your instructor leads you through these activities, you will learn the skills and concepts effectively.

We believe strongly in the instructor-led class. During class, focus on your instructor. Our manuals are designed and written to facilitate your interaction with your instructor, and not to call attention to manuals themselves.

We believe in the basic approach of setting expectations, delivering instruction, and providing summary and review afterwards. For this reason, lessons begin with objectives and end with summaries. We also provide overall course objectives and a course summary to provide both an introduction to and closure on the entire course.

Manual components

The manuals contain these major components:

- Table of contents
- Introduction
- Units
- Course summary
- Quick reference
- Glossary
- Index

Each element is described below.

Table of contents

The table of contents acts as a learning roadmap.

Introduction

The introduction contains information about our training philosophy and our manual components, features, and conventions. It contains target student, prerequisite, objective, and setup information for the specific course.

Units

Units are the largest structural component of the course content. A unit begins with a title page that lists objectives for each major subdivision, or topic, within the unit. Within each topic, conceptual and explanatory information alternates with hands-on activities. Units conclude with a summary comprising one paragraph for each topic, and an independent practice activity that gives you an opportunity to practice the skills you've learned.

The conceptual information takes the form of text paragraphs, exhibits, lists, and tables. The activities are structured in two columns, one telling you what to do, the other providing explanations, descriptions, and graphics.

Course summary

This section provides a text summary of the entire course. It is useful for providing closure at the end of the course. The course summary also indicates the next course in this series, if there is one, and lists additional resources you might find useful as you continue to learn about the software.

Quick reference

The quick reference is an at-a-glance job aid summarizing some of the more common features of the software.

Glossary

The glossary provides definitions for all of the key terms used in this course.

Index

The index at the end of this manual makes it easy for you to find information about a particular software component, feature, or concept.

Manual conventions

We've tried to keep the number of elements and the types of formatting to a minimum in the manuals. This aids in clarity and makes the manuals more classically elegant looking. But there are some conventions and icons you should know about.

Item	Description
Italic text	In conceptual text, indicates a new term or feature.
Bold text	In unit summaries, indicates a key term or concept. In an independent practice activity, indicates an explicit item that you select, choose, or type.
`Code font`	Indicates code or syntax.

`Longer strings of ▶`
`code will look ▶`
`like this.`
	In the hands-on activities, any code that's too long to fit on a single line is divided into segments by one or more continuation characters (▶). This code should be entered as a continuous string of text.

Select **bold item**	In the left column of hands-on activities, bold sans-serif text indicates an explicit item that you select, choose, or type.
Keycaps like ↵ ENTER	Indicate a key on the keyboard you must press.

Hands-on activities

The hands-on activities are the most important parts of our manuals. They are divided into two primary columns. The "Here's how" column gives short instructions to you about what to do. The "Here's why" column provides explanations, graphics, and clarifications. Here's a sample:

Do it!

A-1: Creating a commission formula

Here's how	Here's why
1 Open Sales	This is an oversimplified sales compensation worksheet. It shows sales totals, commissions, and incentives for five sales reps.
2 Observe the contents of cell F4	F4 = =E4*C_Rate The commission rate formulas use the name "C_Rate" instead of a value for the commission rate.

For these activities, we have provided a collection of data files designed to help you learn each skill in a real-world business context. As you work through the activities, you will modify and update these files. Of course, you might make a mistake and therefore want to re-key the activity starting from scratch. To make it easy to start over, you will rename each data file at the end of the first activity in which the file is modified. Our convention for renaming files is to add the word "My" to the beginning of the file name. In the above activity, for example, a file called "Sales" is being used for the first time. At the end of this activity, you would save the file as "My sales," thus leaving the "Sales" file unchanged. If you make a mistake, you can start over using the original "Sales" file.

In some activities, however, it might not be practical to rename the data file. If you want to retry one of these activities, ask your instructor for a fresh copy of the original data file.

Topic B: Setting your expectations

Properly setting your expectations is essential to your success. This topic will help you do that by providing:

- Prerequisites for this course
- A description of the target student
- A list of the objectives for the course
- A skills assessment for the course

Course prerequisites

Before taking this course, you should be familiar with personal computers and the use of a keyboard and a mouse. Furthermore, this course assumes that you've completed the following courses or have equivalent experience:

- *Excel 2007: Basic*
- *Excel 2007: Intermediate*

Target student

You should have some experience with Excel 2007 and should be familiar with intermediate-level tasks, such as sorting data, linking worksheets, and outlining and consolidating data. You'll get the most out of this course if your goal is to become proficient in performing advanced tasks, such as creating nested functions, working with data tables, exporting and importing data, performing what-if analyses, and recording macros.

Microsoft Certified Application Specialist certification

This course is designed to help you pass the Microsoft Certified Application Specialist exam for Excel 2007. For comprehensive certification training, you should complete all of the following courses:

- *Excel 2007: Basic*
- *Excel 2007: Intermediate*
- *Excel 2007: Advanced*

Course objectives

These overall course objectives will give you an idea about what to expect from the course. It is also possible that they will help you see that this course is not the right one for you. If you think you either lack the prerequisite knowledge or already know most of the subject matter to be covered, you should let your instructor know that you think you are misplaced in the class.

Note: In addition to the general objectives listed below, specific Microsoft Certified Application Specialist exam objectives are listed at the beginning of each topic (where applicable). To download a complete mapping of exam objectives to ILT Series content, go to: www.virtualrom.com/658ACD612

After completing this course, you will know how to:

- Use the IF and SUMIF functions to calculate a value based on specified criteria; use a nested IF function to evaluate complex conditions; use the ROUND function to round off numbers; and use the PMT function to calculate periodic payments for a loan.
- Use the VLOOKUP function to find a value in a worksheet list; use the MATCH function to find the relative position of a value in a range; use the INDEX function to find the value of a cell at a given position in a range; and use data tables to project values.
- Use the Data Validation feature to validate data entered in cells; and use database functions to summarize list values that meet criteria you specify.
- Create a PivotTable for analyzing and comparing large amounts of data; change PivotTable views by moving fields and hiding and showing details; improve the appearance of a PivotTable by changing its field settings and applying a style; and create a PivotChart to graphically display data from a PivotTable.
- Export data from Excel to a text file, and import data from a text file into an Excel workbook; import XML data into a workbook, and export data from a workbook to an XML data file; and use Microsoft Query and the Web query feature to import data from external databases.
- Use the Goal Seek and Solver utilities to meet a target output for a formula by adjusting the values in the input cells; install and use the Analysis ToolPak to perform statistical analysis; create scenarios to save various sets of input values that produce different results; and create views to save different sets of worksheet display and print settings.
- Run a macro to perform tasks automatically; record macros; assign a macro to a button, and use the button to run the macro; edit a macro by editing VBA code; and create a custom function to perform calculations when built-in functions are not available.
- Represent data graphically within cells by applying three forms of conditional formatting: data bars, color scales, and icon sets; and insert and modify SmartArt graphics.

Skills inventory

Use the following form to gauge your skill level entering the class. For each skill listed, rate your familiarity from 1 to 5, with five being the most familiar. *This is not a test.* Rather, it is intended to provide you with an idea of where you're starting from at the beginning of class. If you're wholly unfamiliar with all the skills, you might not be ready for the class. If you think you already understand all of the skills, you might need to move on to the next course in the series. In either case, you should let your instructor know as soon as possible.

Skill	1	2	3	4	5
Using the IF, SUMIF, and ROUND functions					
Using the PMT function					
Using the VLOOKUP, MATCH, and INDEX functions					
Using data tables to project values					
Validating data					
Using database functions					
Creating, rearranging, and formatting PivotTables					
Creating PivotCharts					
Importing data from and exporting data to text files					
Importing and exporting XML data					
Using Microsoft Query and Web query					
Using Goal Seek and Solver					
Installing and using the Analysis ToolPak					
Creating scenarios and views					
Running and recording macros					
Editing VBA modules					
Creating custom functions					
Applying conditional formatting to represent data graphically					
Inserting and modifying SmartArt graphics					

Topic C: Re-keying the course

If you have the proper hardware and software, you can re-key this course after class. This section explains what you'll need in order to do so, and how to do it.

Hardware requirements

Your personal computer should have:

- A keyboard and a mouse
- Pentium 500 MHz processor (or higher)
- At least 256 MB RAM
- At least 3 GB of available hard drive space
- CD-ROM drive
- XGA monitor (1024×768 minimum resolution support)
- Internet access, if you want to download the Student Data files, and for downloading the latest updates and service packs from www.windowsupdate.com

Software requirements

You will also need the following software:

- Microsoft Windows XP, Windows Vista, or Windows Server 2003
- Microsoft Office 2007
- Notepad

Network requirements

The following network components and connectivity are also required for rekeying this course:

- Internet access, for the following purposes:
  - Updating the Windows operating system and Microsoft Office 2007 at update.microsoft.com
  - Downloading the Student Data files (if necessary)

Setup instructions to re-key the course

Before you re-key the course, you will need to perform the following steps.

1 Download the latest critical updates and service packs from www.windowsupdate.com.

2 From the Control Panel, open the Display Properties dialog box and apply the following settings:

- Theme — Windows XP
- Screen resolution — 1024 by 768 pixels
- Color quality — High (24 bit) or higher

If you choose not to apply these display settings, your screens might not match the screen shots in this manual.

3 Install Microsoft Office 2007 according to the software manufacturer's instructions, as follows:

a When prompted for the CD key, enter the code included with your software.

b Select the Custom installation option and click Next.

c Clear all check boxes except Microsoft Excel.

d Select "Choose advanced customization of applications" and click Next.

e Next to Microsoft Office Excel for Windows, click the drop-down arrow and choose "Run all from My Computer."

f Next to Office Shared Features, click the drop-down arrow and choose "Run all from My Computer."

g Click Next. Then, click Install to start the installation.

h When the installation has been completed successfully, click Finish.

4 Reset the Quick Access toolbar in Excel.

a Click the Office Button and then click Excel Options.

b Click Customize in the category list.

c Click Reset and then click OK.

5 If necessary, reset other Excel 2007 defaults that you have changed. If you do not wish to reset the defaults, you can still re-key the course, but some activities might not work exactly as documented.

6 Create a folder named Student Data at the root of the hard drive. For a standard hard drive setup, this will be C:\Student Data.

7 Download the Student Data files for the course. (If you do not have an Internet connection, you can ask your instructor for a copy of the data files on a disk.)

a Connect to http://www.courseilt.com/ilt_downloads.cfm.

b Click the link for Microsoft Excel 2007 to display a page of course listings, and then click the link for Excel 2007: Advanced.

c Click the link for downloading the Student Data files, and follow the instructions that appear on your screen.

8 Copy the data files to the Student Data folder.

CertBlaster exam preparation software

If you plan to take the Microsoft Certified Application Specialist exam for Excel 2007, we encourage you to use the CertBlaster pre- and post-assessment software that comes with this course. To download and install your free software:

1. Go to www.courseilt.com/certblaster.
2. Click the link for Excel 2007.
3. Save the .EXE file to a folder on your hard drive. (Note: If you skip this step, the CertBlaster software will not install correctly.)
4. Click Start and choose Run.
5. Click Browse and then navigate to the folder that contains the .EXE file.
6. Select the .EXE file and click Open.
7. Click OK and follow the on-screen instructions. When prompted for the password, enter **c_602**.

Unit 1

Advanced functions

Unit time: 50 minutes

Complete this unit, and you'll know how to:

A Use logical functions to calculate values based on specified criteria, and use nested functions and the ROUND function.

B Use math and statistical functions to conditionally summarize, count, and average data.

C Use the PMT function to calculate periodic payments for a loan.

D Display and print formulas

Topic A: Logical functions

This topic covers the following Microsoft Certified Application Specialist exam objective for Excel 2007.

#	Objective
3.6.1	Using IF, AND, OR, NOT, IFERROR

Conditional logic

Explanation

You can use conditional logic in a formula to return a specific result depending on whether a certain test, or condition, is met. If the condition is true, one result will be calculated. If the condition is false, a difference result will be displayed.

Microsoft Excel 2007 provides several logical functions you can use for conditionally evaluating a calculation: IF, AND, OR, NOT, and IFERROR.

The IF function

The IF function evaluates a condition, or logical test. If the condition is true, the function returns a specific value. Otherwise, it returns another value. The syntax of the IF function is:

```
IF(logical_test,value_if_true,value_if_false)
```

In this syntax, `logical_test` is the criterion you want the function to evaluate, `value_if_true` is the value to be returned if the condition is true, and `value_if_false` is the value to be returned if the condition is false.

Do it!

A-1: Using the IF function

Here's how	Here's why
1 Start Excel	Choose Start, All Programs, Microsoft Office, Microsoft Office Excel 2007.
2 Open Advanced formulas	This workbook contains seven worksheets
3 Save the workbook as **My advanced formulas**	In the current unit folder.
Verify that the If sheet is active	
4 Select G8	You'll use the IF function to calculate the commission for each salesperson. If the total-sales value is greater than the sales-goal value in cell B4, the commission should be calculated as 2% of the total sales. Otherwise, "Not applicable" should appear in the cell.
Type **=IF(F8>$B$4,**	In this function, "F8>$B$4" is the condition that will be evaluated. The reference to B4 is absolute (expressed as $B$4) because you'll AutoFill the cell to the ones below, and the other formulas should all refer to B4.
Type **F8*2%,**	"F8*2%" is the value to be returned if the condition is true.
Type **"NA")**	"NA" is the value to be returned if the condition is false.
Press ENTER	The value NA appears in G8. Because the condition F8>B4 is false ($7,450<$8,500), the value NA is returned.
5 Copy the formula in G8 to G9:G22	(Use the AutoFill handle.) To calculate the remaining commissions.
Observe the Commission column	You'll see the commission amount for each salesperson.
6 Update the workbook	

Creating nested functions

Explanation

You can use nested functions to perform more complex calculations. A *nested function* serves as an argument of another function; in other words, it's contained within another function. For example, an IF function can contain other IF functions as arguments. It can also contain the OR, AND, or NOT functions.

The OR, AND, and NOT functions

OR, AND, and NOT are also functions you can use to conditionally evaluate a formula. While you can use OR, AND, and NOT by themselves, they are more helpful if used within an IF function. You can use the OR, AND, and NOT functions within an IF function in order to determine whether multiple conditions are true, whether some conditions are true, or whether a condition is *not* true. The syntax for these functions, when nested within an IF function, is described below.

The OR function

With the OR function, only *one* of the conditions named needs to be true for the specified result to be displayed. Here's the syntax:

```
IF(OR(logical1,logical2),value_if true,value_if_false)
```

The AND function

In the AND function, *all* conditions specified must be met for the `value_if_true` result to be returned.

```
IF(AND(logical1,logical2),value_if_true,value_if_false)
```

The NOT function

The NOT function reverses the value of its argument. In other words, you state the result you want if the condition specified is not true.

```
IF(NOT(logical),value_if true,value_if_false)
```

Total sales	Commission	Training completed	Year-end bonus	Winner's Circle	Further training
$7,450	NA	No	No bonus		Recommended
$10,260	$257	No	No bonus		
$15,700	$393	No	No bonus		
$12,225	$306	Yes	$183	Yes	
$9,720	$243	Yes	$146		
$7,000	NA	Yes	No bonus		Recommended
$16,840	$421	No	No bonus		
$12,110	$303	Yes	$182	Yes	
$7,790	NA	Yes	No bonus		Recommended
$8,900	$223	No	No bonus		
$6,900	NA	No	No bonus		Recommended
$10,550	$264	Yes	$158		
$14,295	$357	Yes	$214	Yes	
$13,440	$336	No	No bonus		
$6,700	NA	Yes	No bonus		Recommended

Exhibit 1-1: A portion of the worksheet showing the results of function calculations

Do it!

A-2: Using OR, AND, and NOT as nested functions

Here's how	Here's why
1 Activate the NOT, AND, OR worksheet	You'll nest these functions within IF functions to create more complex calculations.
2 In I8, enter **=IF(OR**	To enter the first part of the nested OR function. You'll use this function to determine whether an employee receives a year-end bonus.
Type **(G8="NA",H8="No"),**	To enter the logical tests you will use to perform the calculation.
3 Type **"No bonus",F8*1.5%)**	The complete formula should look like the one shown below.
=IF(OR(G8="NA",H8="No"),"No bonus",F8*1.5%)	
	To enter the values that will be returned if either condition is true.
4 Press ENTER	To complete the formula and calculate the result. "No bonus" appears in the cell.
Copy the formula to I9:I22	
Observe the Year-end bonus column	Many employees do not get a bonus because they did not meet or exceed the sales goal or they did not complete training. Remember that only one of the conditions in the OR function needs to be true in order for the function to return the first specified value, which is "No bonus."
5 Select J8	You'll create a nested AND function to determine which employees belong in the Winner's Circle.
6 Enter the formula shown:	
=IF(AND(H8="Yes",F8>12000),"Yes","")	
	In this formula, both logical tests (conditions) must be true in order to return the first value of "Yes." In other words, an employee must have completed training *and* exceeded $12,000 in total sales in order to be in the Winner's Circle.
7 Copy the formula to J9:J22	Only three employees meet both conditions outlined in the formula: Rebecca Austin, Trevor Johnson, and Sandra Lawrence.
8 Select K8	You'll use a nested NOT function to determine which employees should get more training.

9 Enter the formula shown:

```
=IF(NOT(F8>=$B$4), "Recommended","")
```

In this formula, if the condition specified (F8>=$B$4) is *not* true, the value "Recommended" will be returned; otherwise, the empty string value "" (or blank) is returned.

10 Copy the formula to K9:K22

Five employees did not make the sales goal of $8,500, so further training is recommended. Your worksheet should look like Exhibit 1-1.

Update the workbook

Nested IF functions

Explanation

You use nested IF functions to evaluate multiple conditions. For example, use a second IF function as the `value_if_false` argument of the first IF function.

Do it!

A-3: Using nested IF functions

Here's how	Here's why
1 Activate the Nested If sheet	
Observe the text box in the worksheet	**Sales Commission** Below 5000 — None Between 5000-15000 — 1% Between 15000-25000 — 1.5% Above 25000 — 2% This sheet calculates commissions on a specialty product's sales based on the range in which the employee's sales fall.
2 Select C7	You'll calculate commissions based on the total sales and the various commission rates.
Type **=IF(B7>25000, B7*2%,**	The first IF function is applied when the total-sales value in B7 is greater than 25,000. If this condition is true, the commission is calculated as 2% of the total sales.
Type **IF(B7>15000, B7*1.5%,**	If the first condition (B7>25000) is false, this condition (B7>15000) is evaluated. If it is true, the commission is calculated as 1.5% of the total sales.
3 Type **IF(B7>5000, B7*1%, 0)))**	The complete formula should look like the screen shot shown below.

```
=IF(B7>25000,B7*2%,IF(B7>15000,B7*1.5%,IF(B7>5000,B7*1%,0)))
```

	If both the first condition (B7>25000) and the second condition (B7>15000) are false, this third condition (B7>5000) is evaluated. If this condition is true, the commission is calculated as 1% of total sales. If this final condition is false, 0 (zero) is returned.
Press ENTER	Because B7 (12,450) is greater than 5000 but less than 15,000, a 1% commission is calculated, and the value $124.50 appears in C7.
4 Copy the formula in C7 to C8:C21	To calculate the remaining commissions.
5 Update the workbook	

The IFERROR function

Explanation

You can use the IFERROR function to check a formula for errors and to replace Excel's default error message with a message you specify. For example, if you try to divide a number by zero in a formula, the error message #DIV/0! appears in the cell by default. You can replace this message with your own by using IFERROR.

The syntax for the IFERROR function is:

```
=IFERROR(value,value_if_error)
```

where `value` is the argument you want to check for an error, and `value_if_error` is the message you want to display if an error is found. If no error is found in the formula, the result of the formula is displayed.

Do it!

A-4: Using the IFERROR function

Here's how	Here's why
1 Activate the IFERROR sheet	You'll use the IFERROR function to find calculation errors and identify them with your own error message.
2 Select D7	
Type **=IFERROR(**	To begin the IFERROR function.
Type **B7/C7,**	To enter the value you want the function to calculate and check for errors.
3 Type **"Check price")**	To specify the error message to display should the function find an error.
Press ENTER	To complete the formula and calculate a result for D7.
4 Copy the formula in D7 to D8:D19	The error message "Check price" appears in D8 and D17 because the formula tried to divide a number by zero.
5 Update the workbook	

Topic B: Math and statistical functions

This topic covers the following Microsoft Certified Application Specialist exam objective for Excel 2007.

#	Objective
3.4.1	**Using SUMIF, SUMIFS, COUNTIF, COUNTIFS, AVERAGEIF, AVERAGEIFS**

Using math and statistical functions

Explanation

You can conditionally summarize, count, and average data by using math and statistical functions. Some of these functions include SUMIF, COUNTIF, AVERAGEIF and SUMIFS, COUNTIFS, and AVERAGEIFS.

The SUMIF function

You use the SUMIF function when you want to add values within a range of cells based on the evaluation of a criterion in another range.

The syntax of the SUMIF function is:

```
SUMIF(range,criteria,sum_range)
```

In this syntax, `range` is the range in which the function will test the criterion specified in `criteria`. The argument `sum_range` specifies the actual cells whose values are to be added. `Sum_range` is optional; if it's omitted, the cells specified in `range` are evaluated by `criteria` and are added if they match `criteria`.

Do it!

B-1: Using SUMIF

Here's how	Here's why
1 Activate the SumIf sheet	
2 Select B29	You'll sum up the sales for the East region for the prior year.
Type **=SUMIF(Region,**	In the formula, "Region" is the named range of cells B8:B22, which SUMIF will evaluate.
Type **"East",**	"East" is the evaluation criterion. You must include quotes around this value because it is a label.
Type **Sales_prior)**	"Sales_prior" is the range C8:C22, which will be summed based on the criterion.
Press ENTER	The value of the East region's total sales for the prior year, $43,685.00, appears in B29.
3 In B30, display the East region's total sales for the current year	(Use the name of the range D8:D22, Sales_current, in the SUMIF function.) The value $56,320.00 appears.
4 In E29, display the North region's total sales for the prior year	(Specify the evaluation criterion as North.) The value $65,040.00 appears.
5 In E30, display the North region's total sales for the current year	The value $70,950.00 appears.
6 Fill in the current and prior years' sales information for the South and West regions	
7 Update the workbook	

The COUNTIF function

Explanation

You use the COUNTIF function to count the number of cells in a range that meet your specified criteria. The syntax for the COUNTIF function is:

```
COUNTIF(range,criteria)
```

`Range` is the cell or range of cells to count that meet the stated criterion. Text values and blank cells are ignored. `Criteria` can be text, numbers, expressions, or cell references that identify the cells to be counted.

Do it!

B-2: Using COUNTIF

Here's how	Here's why
1 Activate G8	You'll count the number of stores that have met or exceeded the current year's sales goal of $15,000.
2 Type **=COUNTIF(**	To start the function.
Type **Sales_current,**	To designate the range in which you will count the cells that meet your criterion.
Type **">=15000")**	To specify the criterion to be met.
3 Press ENTER	To complete the function and return the result. The value 9 appears in the cell because there are nine stores meeting or exceeding the sales goal.
4 Update the workbook	

The AVERAGEIF function

Explanation

AVERAGEIF is, like SUMIF and COUNTIF, a conditional math function. Use AVERAGEIF to conditionally average a range of numbers.

The syntax for the AVERAGEIF function is:

```
AVERAGEIF(range,criteria,average_range)
```

`Range` is the cell or range of cells you want to average, `criteria` is the number, expression, cell reference, or text that identifies which cells should be averaged. `Average_range` is the corresponding set of cells you want to average. If you omit this, `range` will be used instead.

Do it!

B-3: Using AVERAGEIF

Here's how	Here's why
1 Activate B31	You'll calculate the average of current-year sales for the East region.
2 Type **=AVERAGEIF(**	To begin the function.
Type **Region,"East",**	To designate Region as the range, and East as the criterion for that range.
Type **Sales_current)**	To designate Sales_current as the range from which the actual cells to be averaged will be drawn.
3 Press ENTER	To finish the function and calculate the result. Cell B31displays $14,080.00, which is the average of current-year sales for the East region.
4 Calculate the average of current-year sales for the remaining regions	
5 Update the workbook	

SUMIFS, COUNTIFS, and AVERAGEIFS

Explanation

Although SUMIF, COUNTIF, and AVERAGEIF are useful for conditionally summarizing data, they allow the use of only one criterion. To remedy this limitation, Microsoft Excel 2007 features the new functions SUMIFS, COUNTIFS, and AVERAGEIFS, which enable you to easily sum, count, and average values in a range using multiple criteria.

The SUMIFS function

The syntax for the SUMIFS function is:

```
SUMIF(sum_range,criteria_range1,criteria1,criteria_range2,
criteria2)
```

`Sum_range` is the cell or range to sum. `Criteria_range1` and `criteria_range2` are the ranges in which the function evaluates the related criteria; `criteria1` and `criteria2` are the actual criteria. Note that in the SUMIFS function, the `sum_range` argument appears first (rather than last, as in SUMIF).

The COUNTIFS function

The syntax for the COUNTIFS function is:

```
COUNTIFS(range1,criteria1,range2,criteria2)
```

`Range1` and `range2` are the ranges where the related criteria are evaluated. `Criteria1` and `criteria2` are the criteria by which the cells or ranges are evaluated.

The AVERAGEIFS function

The syntax for the AVERAGEIFS function is:

```
AVERAGEIFS(average_range,criteria_range1,criteria1,
criteria_range2,criteria2)
```

`Average_range` is the range of cells to average, while `criteria_range1` and `criteria_range2` are the ranges where the function evaluates the related criteria. `Criteria1` and `criteria2` are the criteria by which the specified cells will be evaluated.

Do it!

B-4: Using SUMIFS, COUNTIFS, and AVERAGEIFS

Here's how	Here's why
1 Activate B32	You'll use the SUMIFS function to sum the increase in sales over the target goal for stores in the East region.
2 Type =**SUMIFS(**	To begin the function.
Type **E8:E22,**	To specify the range containing the cells to be summarized.
Type **Region,"East",**	To specify the first criteria range and the first criterion by which to evaluate the range.
Type **Sales_current,">15000")**	To specify the second criteria range and the second criterion.
3 Press ENTER	To enter the function. The value $6,985.00 is displayed. This is the total of the increase in sales over the target goal for all stores in the East region.
4 Calculate the increase in sales above the target goal for the remaining regions	
5 Activate B33	You'll calculate the number of stores in the East region that exceeded the target sales goal.
Type **=COUNTIFS(**	To begin the function.
6 Type **Region,"East",**	To specify the first range and the criterion by which the range will be evaluated.
Type **Sales_current,">15000")**	To specify the second range and the criterion by which it will be evaluated.
7 Press ENTER	To complete the function and display the result. Two stores in the East region exceeded the sales target of $15,000.
Calculate the number of stores exceeding the target sales goal in each of the remaining regions	
8 Select B34	You'll use the AVERAGEIFS function to calculate the average increase in sales for those stores exceeding the target goal.

9 Type **=AVERAGEIFS(**	To begin the function.
Type **E8:E22,**	To specify the range containing the cells to be averaged.
Type **Region,"East",**	To specify the first criteria range and the first criterion.
10 Type **Sales_current,">15000")**	To specify the second criteria range and the second criterion.
Press ENTER	To complete the function and display the result. $3,492.50 appears in B34.
11 Calculate the average increase in sales for the remaining regions	
Update the workbook	

The ROUND function

Explanation

You can round off a value to a specified number of digits by using the ROUND function. The syntax of the ROUND function is:

```
ROUND(value,num_digits)
```

The first argument of the function is the value you want to round off. The second argument is the number of digits to which you want to round off that value. If `num_digits` is positive, the function rounds off the number to the specified number of decimal places. However, if `num_digits` is negative, the function rounds off the value to the left of the decimal point. For example, `ROUND(126.87,1)` returns 126.9, and `ROUND(126.87,-1)` returns 130.

Evaluation order of conditions

You might want to view the evaluation order of the conditions in a function to understand that function. To view the evaluation order:

1. Select the cell containing the function you want to evaluate. You can evaluate only one cell at a time.
2. In the Formula Auditing group on the Formulas tab, click the Evaluate Formula button to open the Evaluate Formula dialog box, shown in Exhibit 1-2.
3. Click Step In to view the value in the selected cell.
4. Click Step Out to return to the function.
5. Click Evaluate to evaluate the underlined part of the function.
6. Click Close.

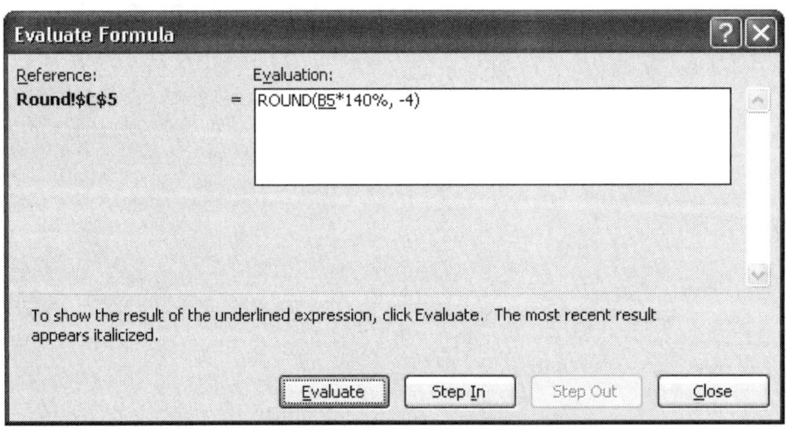

Exhibit 1-2: The Evaluate Formula dialog box

Do it!

B-5: Using ROUND

Here's how	Here's why
1 Activate the Round sheet	
2 Select C5	You'll calculate the target sales for Atlanta.
Enter **=B5*140%**	The target sales figure for the current year is calculated as 140% of the total sales for the prior year. The value $9,778,688.92 appears. You'll round the value in C5.
3 Edit C5 to read **=ROUND(B5*140%,-4)**	In this formula, "B5*140%" is the value to be rounded, and "-4" specifies that four digits to the left of the decimal point should be rounded. In other words, the value should be rounded to the ten-thousands place.
Press ENTER	The value $9,780,000.00 is displayed.
4 Copy the formula in C5 to C6:C18	To round off the target sales values for the remaining cities.
5 Select C5	You'll determine the order in which the ROUND function's components are evaluated.
6 Activate the Formulas tab	
7 In the Formula Auditing group, click **Evaluate Formula**	To open the Evaluate Formula dialog box, shown in Exhibit 1-2. The ROUND function appears in the Evaluation box. In the function, B5 is underlined, indicating that the value in this cell is used to evaluate the function.
8 Click **Step In**	To view the current value in B5, which is $6,984,777.80.
9 Click **Step Out**	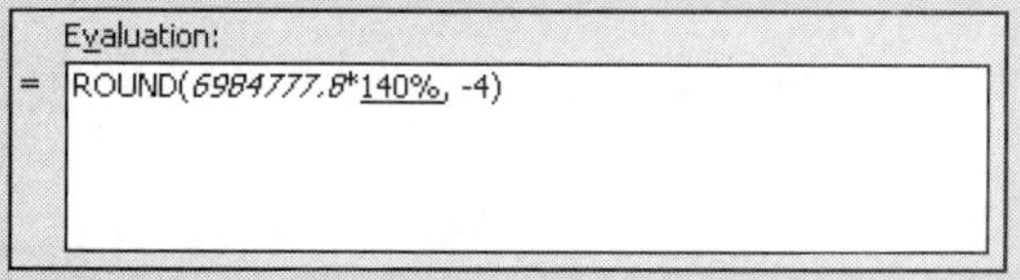 To return to the formula. In the formula, B5 has been replaced by its current value. Notice that 140% is underlined, indicating that it will be evaluated next.

10 Click **Evaluate**	In the formula, 1.4 replaces 140%. The first argument of the ROUND function is underlined, indicating that it will be evaluated next.
Click **Evaluate**	The result of evaluation, 9778688.92, appears. The entire ROUND function is underlined. This indicates that the value 9778688.92 will be rounded off next.
Click **Evaluate**	The value $9,780,000.00 appears.
11 Click **Close**	To close the Evaluate Formula dialog box.
12 Update the workbook	

Topic C: Financial functions

Explanation

Excel provides several financial functions for calculating such values as depreciation, future or present loan values, and loan payments. One financial function is the PMT function, which you can use to calculate loan payments.

The PMT function

The PMT function returns the periodic payments for a loan. The return value is negative if the amount is to be paid, and positive if the amount is to be obtained.

The syntax of the PMT function is:

```
PMT(rate,nper,pv,fv,type)
```

The following table describes each argument of the PMT function:

Argument	Description
`rate`	The interest rate per period. For example, if you get a loan at 10% annual interest and you make monthly payments, the first argument will be 10%/12.
`nper`	The number of payments that have to be made to repay the loan. For example, if you have four years to pay back the loan, and you make monthly payments, the second argument will be 48 (4*12).
`pv`	The present value, or the principal amount of the loan. This argument can also have a negative value. For example, if you give a loan of $12,000, the present value will be -12000. However, if you take a loan of $12,000, the present value will be 12000.
`fv`	(Optional.) The future value of the loan—that is, its value after the last payment is made. If you omit the future value, it's assumed to be zero.
`type`	(Optional.) Indicates when payments are due. This argument can have either of two values: 0 if payments are due at the end of the period, or 1 if payments are due at the beginning of the period. If you omit this argument, it's assumed to be zero.

Do it!

C-1: Using the PMT function

Here's how	Here's why
1 Activate the PMT sheet	
2 Select E6	You'll calculate the monthly payment to be made to AmericaBank.
Type **=PMT(D6%/12,**	In this formula, "D6%/12" is the monthly rate of interest.
Type **C6,B6)**	*fx* =PMT(D6%/12,C6,B6) "C6" refers to the cell containing the period of repayment, and "B6" refers to the cell containing the present value of the loan.
Press ENTER	The value -$3,417.76 appears in E6. The negative sign signifies that you have to pay this amount.
3 Copy the formula in E6 to E7:E8 and E10:E11	To calculate the monthly payments for the remaining banks.
4 Change the value in C6 to **24**	Notice the changes in the monthly payment.
5 Update the workbook	

Topic D: Displaying and printing formulas

This topic covers the following Microsoft Certified Application Specialist exam objective for Excel 2007.

#	Objective
3.8	Display and print formulas

Viewing formulas in a worksheet

Explanation

You can display the formulas in a worksheet rather than their results. This is helpful when you want to audit your formulas. There are two ways to display formulas in a worksheet:

- On the Formulas tab, in the Formula Auditing group, click Show Formulas.
- Press Ctrl +` (grave accent).

Once the formulas are displayed in a worksheet, they can also be printed. To display the formula results again, click Show Formulas or press Ctrl + `.

Hiding formulas

There's a difference between not displaying formulas and hiding them. When you choose not to display formulas, the formula will still appear in the formula bar when you select the cell that shows that formula's result.

You can also hide formulas from users. This is useful when you want to prevent the formulas from being edited. A hidden formula will not be shown in the formula bar even when the associated cell is selected.

To hide a formula:

1. Select the cells whose formulas you want to hide. These can be adjacent or not, and you can select the whole sheet.
2. On the Home tab, in the Cells group, click Format and choose Format Cells.
3. Activate the Protection tab, check Hidden, and click OK.
4. On the Home tab, in the Cells group, click Format and choose Protect Sheet.
5. Ensure that the "Protect worksheet and contents of locked cells" check box is selected.
6. Click OK.

To show formulas that were previously hidden, you remove protection. Here's how:

1. On the Review tab, in the Changes group, click Unprotect Sheet.
2. Select the range of cells whose formulas you want to unhide.
3. On the Home tab, in the Cells group, click Format and choose Format Cells.
4. Activate the Protection tab, clear the Hidden check box, and click OK.

Do it!

D-1: Showing, printing, and hiding formulas

Here's how	Here's why
1 Activate the ROUND sheet	You'll display the formulas in this sheet.
2 Select C5	
Observe the formula bar	It shows the formula, while E5 shows the result of that formula.
3 Press CTRL + `	(The accent grave is usually to the left of the number 1 on the keyboard.) To display formulas in the cells.
Observe the Target sales column	It shows the formulas instead of the results.
4 Click 	
Choose **Print**, **Print Preview**	
Observe the Target sales column in the print preview	(Move to the second page and zoom in, if necessary.) Formulas are shown instead of the formulas' results. This can be handy for auditing the formulas.
Click **Close Print Preview**	You won't print at this time.
5 Show the formulas in the cells	If necessary.
6 Select column C5 to C18	You'll hide the formulas in these cells.
7 On the Home tab, in the Cells group, click **Format** and choose **Format Cells**	To open the Custom Lists dialog box.
Activate the Protection tab	If necessary.
Check **Hidden**	Note that this setting will not take effect until you protect the sheet.
Click **OK**	To close the Custom Lists dialog box and return to the worksheet.
8 On the Review tab, in the Changes group, click **Protect Sheet**	To open the Protect Sheet dialog box.
Check **Protect worksheet and contents of locked cells**	If necessary.
Click **OK**	To close the Protect Sheet dialog box.

9	Select C5	You'll test to see if the cell has been locked.
	Observe the formula bar	The formula does not appear.
10	Try to edit the cell	Press any letter or number while the cell is selected. A message appears, telling you that the cell is protected and therefore read-only.
	Click **OK**	To close the message box.
11	Unprotect the sheet	On the Review tab, in the Changes group, click Unprotect Sheet.
	Observe the formula bar	You can see the formula in C5.
12	Close the workbook	Don't save the latest changes.

Unit summary: Advanced functions

Topic A

In this topic, you learned how to use the **logical functions** IF, AND, OR, and NOT to evaluate a condition and return a value based on whether that condition is true or false. You also learned how to use **nested functions** to perform complex calculations. You learned that a nested IF function can be used to evaluate multiple conditions. Finally, you learned how to use the IFERROR function.

Topic B

In this topic, you learned how to use the **math and statistical functions** SUMIF, SUMIFS, COUNTIF, COUNTIFS, AVERAGEIF, and AVERAGEIFS to conditionally summarize, count, and average data. You also learned how to round off a number by using the ROUND function. In addition, you learned how to view the **evaluation order** of the conditions in a function by using the Evaluate Formula dialog box.

Topic C

In this topic, you learned how to use the PMT function to calculate periodic payments for a loan.

Topic D

In this topic, you learned how to display, print, and hide formulas.

Independent practice activity

In this activity, you'll specify calculations, such as a nested IF function.

1 Open Advanced formulas practice.

2 Save the workbook as **My advanced formulas practice**.

3 Use a nested IF function to determine the performance grade for each salesperson based on the percent increase in sales. For example, if the percent increase in sales is above 25%, the grade will be A, and so on. The criteria for all performance grades are given in the following table. (*Hint:* Scroll down to cell A100 to see the correct formula.)

Increase	Grade
Above 25%	A
15%–25%	B
0%–15%	C
Below 0%	D

4 Activate the Loan statement worksheet and calculate the quarterly amount to be paid to all the institutions. (*Hint:* You'll need to divide the interest rate by 4 instead of 12. Scroll down to cell A101 to see the correct formula.) Copy the formula to E6:E9. If necessary, increase the column width to see the results fully.

5 Compare your results with Exhibit 1-3.

6 Update the workbook.

7 Display the formulas in the cells.

8 Examine the formulas in Print Preview. Close the Print Preview when you're done.

9 Display the results of the formulas in the cells again.

10 Hide the formulas from users. (*Hint*: You need to format these cells as hidden and then protect the worksheet.) Test that the formulas are hidden and that you can't edit the cells.

11 Unprotect the worksheet.

12 Close the workbook without saving.

	A	B	C	D	E
2			Statement of loan		
3					
4	**Institution**	**Loan amount (in $)**	**Period of repayment (in quarters)**	**Annual Rate of Interest (in %)**	**Quarterly payment**
5	AmericaBank	$150,000	12	14	-$15,522.59
6	NewCiti	$325,000	16	15	-$27,379.57
7	StandardBank	$375,000	20	10	-$24,055.17
8	DoubleMoney	$450,000	20	15	-$32,382.94
9	WACA	$635,000	24	10	-$35,504.64
10	**Total**	$1,935,000			

Exhibit 1-3: The Loan statement worksheet after Step 6 of the independent practice activity

Review questions

1 What is the syntax of the IF function?

2 What is a nested function?

3 If you want to view the evaluation order of a complex function, you can use the Evaluate Formula dialog box. How do you open this dialog box?

4 What function returns the periodic payments for a loan?

Unit 2

Lookups and data tables

Unit time: 50 minutes

Complete this unit, and you'll know how to:

A Use the VLOOKUP and HLOOKUP functions to find values in a worksheet list.

B Use the MATCH function to find the relative position of a value in a range, and use the INDEX function to find the value of a cell at a given position within a range.

C Use data tables to see the effects of changing the values in a formula.

Topic A: Using lookup functions

This topic covers the following Microsoft Certified Application Specialist exam objective for Excel 2007.

#	Objective
3.5.1	**Includes: VLOOKUP, HLOOKUP** • Use VLOOKUP to locate values associated with an exact match (FALSE). • Use VLOOKUP to locate a cell in a list that has the value closest to the target value (TRUE). • Use HLOOKUP to locate values associated with an exact match (FALSE). • Use HLOOKUP to locate a cell in a list that has the value closest to the target value (TRUE).

HLOOKUP and VLOOKUP

You can find a value in a range of related data in a worksheet by using *lookup functions*. These functions find a value in the first row or column of a list and then return a corresponding value from another row or column.

The HLOOKUP function performs a horizontal lookup. It finds values in a lookup table that has row labels in the leftmost column. The VLOOKUP function performs a vertical lookup. It finds values in a lookup table that has column labels in the topmost row.

HLOOKUP searches for the lookup value in the first row of the lookup table and returns a value in the same column from the specified row of the table. The syntax is:

```
HLOOKUP(lookup_value,table_array,row_index_num,range_lookup)
```

In this syntax:

- `lookup_value` is located in the first row of the lookup table.
- `table_array` is the name of the lookup table range.
- `row_index_num` is the number of the row from which a value will be returned.
- `range_lookup` is an optional argument that specifies whether you want HLOOKUP to find an exact or approximate match. You can specify FALSE if you want the function to search for a value that falls within a range, or specify TRUE if you want the function to search for an approximate match. If you omit the argument, HLOOKUP assumes that the value is TRUE.

Similarly, VLOOKUP searches for the lookup value in the first column of the lookup table and returns a value in the same row from the specified column of the table. The syntax is:

```
VLOOKUP(lookup_value,table_array,col_index_num,range_lookup)
```

In this syntax:

- `lookup_value` is located in the first column of the lookup table.
- `table_array` is the name of the lookup table range.

- `col_index_num` is the number of the column from which a value will be returned.
- `range_lookup` is an optional argument that specifies whether you want VLOOKUP to find an exact or approximate match. If you omit the argument, VLOOKUP assumes that the value is TRUE.

Do it!

A-1: Examining VLOOKUP

Here's how	Here's why
1 Open Lookups	(From the current unit folder.) This workbook contains seven worksheets; Lookup is the active sheet. The data in the Lookup worksheet is sorted in ascending order by the values in the Employee ID column. The range A4:E6 contains a search box that currently displays the name and department for the employee identification number E001.
2 Save the workbook as **My lookups**	In the current unit folder.
3 Verify that sheet Lookup is active	
In A6, enter **E037**	The name and department details of Employee ID E037 appear in B6 and C6, respectively. Entering an incorrect identification number in A6 would create errors in B6 and C6.
4 Select B6	It contains a VLOOKUP function that finds the name of the employee whose identification number is specified in A6.
Observe the formula bar	*fx* =VLOOKUP(A6,Emp_info,2,FALSE) In this formula, "A6" refers to the cell containing the value that the function has to find. "Emp_info" is the range A10:F49, which constitutes the lookup table. The "2" refers to the table column from which the matching value is returned. "FALSE" indicates that the function must find an exact match. In the row containing E037, the value in the second column of the lookup table is Davis Lee.
5 Select C6	*fx* =VLOOKUP(A6,Emp_info,5,FALSE) It contains a VLOOKUP function that finds the department of the person whose employee identification number appears in A6.
6 Update the workbook	

Use VLOOKUP for exact matches

Explanation

When you use the VLOOKUP function, remember the following:

- The lookup value must always be located in the first column of the lookup table.
- If the `range_lookup` argument is TRUE, the values in the first column of the lookup range must be in ascending order.
- Uppercase and lowercase text are equivalent.

Do it!

A-2: Using VLOOKUP to find an exact match

Here's how	Here's why
1 Select D6	You'll use the VLOOKUP function to find the earnings of the employee whose ID is entered in A6.
Enter **=VLOOKUP(A6,Emp_info,6,FALSE)**	The value 72500 appears.
2 In E6, enter **=VLOOKUP(A6,Emp_info,4,FALSE)**	The value East appears. This is the region of the employee whose ID is entered in A6.
3 In A6, enter **E029**	The name, department, earnings, and region of Employee ID E029 appear in the corresponding cells.
4 Update the workbook	

Use VLOOKUP for approximate matches

Explanation

You can also use the VLOOKUP function to return an approximate match. To do this, specify the `range_lookup` argument as TRUE. If the function doesn't find an exact match, it looks for the largest value that is less than the lookup value and returns its corresponding data. This is also the default value if you leave the argument blank.

If the lookup value is less than the smallest value in the table, an error (#N/A) is returned.

Do it!

A-3: Using VLOOKUP to find an approximate match

Here's how	Here's why
1 Activate the Vlookup sheet	This table lists discount percentages corresponding to purchase amounts. Because there are so many levels of discounts, it would be impractical to calculate the percentage with a large nested IF function. Instead, you'll find the nearest discount percentage based on an approximate matching lookup.
2 Select B6	You'll use the VLOOKUP function to find the discount percentage for the amount entered in A6. The table correlating purchase amounts to discounts is named Discount_table.
Enter **=VLOOKUP(A6,Discount_table,2,TRUE)**	
	Because the value in A6 is $1000, the lookup formula in B6 results in 3%, matching the data in the lookup table.
	You'll now enter a purchase amount value that doesn't appear in the table. The TRUE value in the last argument of the function tells VLOOKUP to look for an approximate match instead of an exact match.
3 In A6, enter **2500**	The discount for a $2000 purchase is 10%, and the discount for a $3500 purchase is 12%. The largest amount value in the lookup table below your entry of $2500 is $2000, so the discount should be 10%. Because the VLOOKUP function is looking for an approximate match, it determines this and returns a discount value of 10%.
4 Update the workbook	

Use HLOOKUP for exact matches

Explanation

HLOOKUP works like VLOOKUP except that it searches for values along a row instead of down a column. When you use the HLOOKUP function, remember the following:

- The lookup value must always be located in the first row of the lookup table.
- If the `range_lookup` argument is TRUE (approximate search), the values in the first column of the lookup range must be in ascending order.
- Uppercase and lowercase text are equivalent.

Do it!

A-4: Using HLOOKUP for exact matches

Here's how	Here's why
1 Activate the HLOOKUP-Exact sheet	You'll add formulas for horizontal lookups.
2 Select B5	A drop-down arrow appears.
3 Click the drop-down arrow and select Qtr2	Corresponding data is displayed in C5. The list ensures that you enter valid data.
4 Select C5	
Observe the formula	It is similar to the VLOOKUP formula, but it searches the first row in table_array rather than the first column.
5 Select D5	
Enter **=HLOOKUP(B5,total_sales,9,FALSE)**	The row_index is 9, which is the row for Net profit. FALSE indicates a search for an exact match.
6 Select E5	
Enter the formula to show Profit % in E5 for the selected quarter	Enter =HLOOKUP(B5,total_sales,10,FALSE). The row_index for Profit % is 10.

Use HLOOKUP for approximate matches

Explanation

You can also use the HLOOKUP function to return an approximate match. To do this, specify the `range_lookup` argument as TRUE. As with VLOOKUP, if the HLOOKUP function doesn't find an exact match, it looks for the largest value that is less than the lookup value and returns its corresponding data. This is also the default value if you leave the argument blank.

If the lookup value is less than the smallest value in the table, an error (#N/A) is returned. The data in the first row must be in ascending order. If it's not, the function might return unexpected results.

Do it!

A-5: Using HLOOKUP for approximate matches

Here's how	Here's why
1 Activate the HLOOKUP-Approx sheet	
2 Select C4	
Enter **=HLOOKUP(B4,base_salary,2,TRUE)**	TRUE indicates an approximate search.
3 Select B4	
Enter an amount between 60,000 and 80,000	You don't need to enter the comma or dollar sign. The function finds the largest value that is less than or equal to the entered value and returns the corresponding name.

Topic B: Using MATCH and INDEX

Explanation

The MATCH and INDEX functions are considered Reference functions. You can use the MATCH function to determine the relative position of a value in a range. Conversely, the INDEX function returns a cell's value based on its relative position in a range. You can combine these two functions to obtain any information from any table.

The MATCH function

The syntax of the MATCH function is:

```
MATCH(lookup_value,lookup_array,match_type)
```

The arguments are:

- `lookup_value` — The value you want to find.
- `lookup_array` — The range of cells containing possible lookup values.
- `match_type` — An optional argument that can have the values 0, 1, or -1. If you want an exact match, specify 0. If you want the function to search for the largest value that is less than or equal to the lookup value, specify 1. If you want the function to search for the smallest value that is greater than or equal to the lookup value, specify -1. If you specify 1, the range should be sorted in ascending order. If you specify -1, the range should be sorted in descending order. If you omit the argument, the function assumes that the value is 1.

Do it!

B-1: Using the MATCH function

Here's how	Here's why
1 Activate the Match and Index sheet	The data appears in ascending order of earnings. You'll use the MATCH function to find the relative position of a value in the selected range. The ranges A4:B6 and E4:F6 contain search boxes.
2 Select B6	You'll find the relative position of "Adam Long" in the column of names.
Enter **=MATCH(B5,Emp_name,0)**	In this formula, "B5" refers to the cell containing the lookup value. "Emp_name" refers to the range B10:B49, where the function searches for the lookup value, and "0" indicates that the values in the search range should match the lookup value exactly.
	The value 4 appears in B6. This is the relative position of "Sandy Stewart" in the column of names. In other words, her name is the fourth name in the list.
3 Select F6	You'll find the relative position of the value in F5 within the range F10:F49, named Earnings.
Enter **=MATCH(F5,Earnings,1)**	In this formula, "1" indicates that the function will find the largest value that is less than or equal to the lookup value.
	The relative position of the value in F5 appears as 24 in F6. In other words, there are 24 values less than or equal to $100,000.
Observe the Earnings column	It doesn't contain the value $100,000. However, MATCH still displays a relative position in F6. This occurs because MATCH returns the relative position of the largest value that's less than or equal to $100,000.
4 Update the workbook	

The INDEX function

Explanation

You can use the INDEX function if you want to find a value in a range by specifying a row number and a column number. The syntax of the INDEX function is:

```
INDEX(range,row_num,col_num)
```

The arguments are:

- `range` — The group of cells in which to look for the value.
- `row_num` — The row from which a value will be returned. If the specified range contains only one row, you can omit the row number.
- `col_num` — The column from which a value will be returned. If the specified range contains only one column, you can omit the column number.

For example, `INDEX(A1:F10,4,6)` returns the value in row 4 and column 6 of the range A1:F10.

By itself, the INDEX function isn't very useful; the person looking for data isn't likely to know the row and column values to enter. When used with the MATCH function, however, the INDEX function can return values that the VLOOKUP function can't. VLOOKUP always looks for a matching value in the *leftmost* column of a data range. If you want to match a value in another column, you can use the MATCH function to return the row that matches the user's input, and then use that result in an INDEX function.

For example, in Exhibit 2-1, cell B6 contains a MATCH function to determine the row for the name entered in B5. Sandy Stewart is the fourth name in the Emp_info list. Cell B7 contains an INDEX function that looks in the row specified in B6 (in this case, row 4) and returns the value of the sixth column (Earnings, in this case, $65,000).

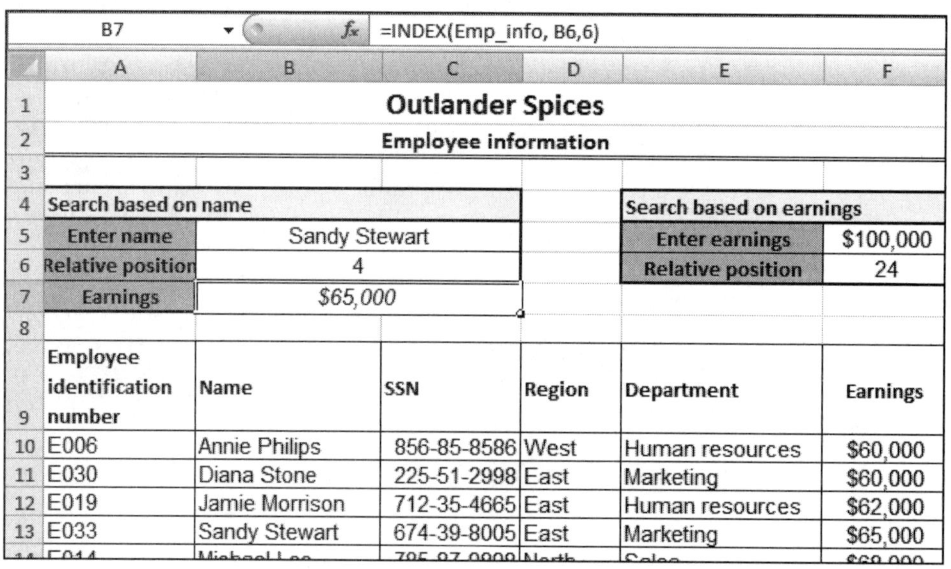

Exhibit 2-1: The INDEX function used with the MATCH function

Do it!

B-2: Using the INDEX function

Here's how	Here's why
1 Observe B7	You want to display the salary for the employee whose name is entered in cell B5. You can't use the VLOOKUP function for this because the person's name is in the second column of the data table, not the first column. You'll begin by experimenting with the INDEX function, which you'll use to solve this problem.
Select B7	You'll enter row and column values directly into the formula this time, to see how the INDEX function works.
Enter **=INDEX(Emp_info,2,6)**	In this formula, "Emp_info" refers to the range A10:F49. The "2" and "6" refer to the row and column from which the function should return a value. The value $60,000 appears in B7. This is the value from the second row and sixth column of the specified range. You'll now replace the number 2 with the value of cell B6, which represents the row of the entered name (calculated by using the MATCH function).
2 Select B7	
Edit the formula to read **=INDEX(Emp_info,B6,6)**	The value $65,000 appears in B7. Because B6 contains the value 4 (the row number for Sandy Stewart), the value in column 6 that the INDEX function returns is her salary.
3 Select B5	You'll verify that the functions work when you enter a different name.
Enter **Davis Lee**	The MATCH function in B6 calculates the relative position of 8, and the INDEX function in B7 calculates the salary of $72,500.
4 Update the workbook	

Topic C: Creating data tables

Explanation

A *data table* is a range that displays the results of changing certain values in one or more formulas. The different values you want to enter in a formula are also included in the data table. A data table can have either a single variable or two variables.

One-variable data tables

You can use a one-variable data table to observe the effects of changing one variable in one or more formulas. For example, you can see how changing the interest rate affects monthly payments in the function `PMT(A5%/12,36,12000)`. In this function, A5 is called the *input cell*, where various input values are substituted from the data table.

To create a one-variable data table:

1 Enter input values in a row or a column.
2 If you list the input values in a column, then enter the formula in the cell located at the intersection of the row above the first input value and the column to the right of the input values, as shown in Exhibit 2-2. If you list the input values in a row, then enter the formula in the cell located at the intersection of the column to the left of the first value and the row just below the row of input values.
3 Select the range containing the input values and the formula.
4 On the Data tab, in the Data Tools group, click What-If Analysis and choose Data Table to open the Table dialog box.
5 If the input values are in a column, specify the input cell in the Column input cell box. If the input values are in a row, use the Row input cell box.
6 Click OK.

Payment analysis	
No. of monthly payments	Monthly payment
See left table	=PMT(B5/12,B6,B7)
6	
12	
18	
24	
30	
36	
42	
48	
54	
60	
66	
72	
78	
84	
90	

Formula (in the row above the first input value and one column to the right of the input values)

Input values

Exhibit 2-2: Creating a one-variable data table

Do it!

C-1: Creating a one-variable data table

Here's how	Here's why
1 Activate the 1v data table sheet	You'll create a one-variable data table to analyze payments. D6:E21 will form the data table. The range D7:D21 contains the input values you'll use while creating the data table.
2 In E6 enter **=PMT(B5/12,B6,B7)**	To calculate monthly payments based on the input cell. The value -8,791.59 appears.
3 Select D6:E21	
4 Activate the Data tab	
In the Data Tools group, click **What-If Analysis**	To display a menu.
Choose **Data Table...**	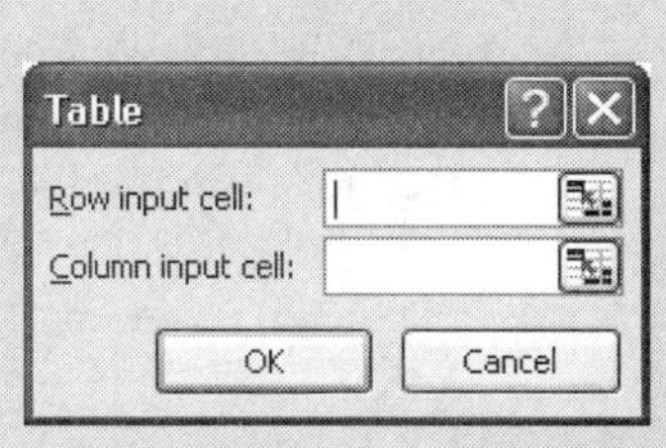 To open the Data Table dialog box. Here, you can specify the row and column input cells.
5 Place the insertion point in the Column input cell box	
Select B6	(In the worksheet.) This is the cell where the list of column input values from the data table will be substituted.
6 Click **OK**	(In the Data Table dialog box.) E6:E21 shows how different values for "No. of monthly payments" affect the monthly payment for the loan amount in B7. Because 12 appears in both the initial formula and the data table, the payment value of –8,791.59 appears twice. You can change the initial value used in the formula without affecting the data table.
In B6, enter **10**	The value in E6 (at the top of the data table) changes to –10,464.04, but the rest of the table values remain.
7 Update the workbook	

Two-variable data tables

Explanation

You can use a two-variable data table to see the effect of changing two variables in one or more formulas, as shown in Exhibit 2-3. For example, you can see how changing the interest rate and the number of payments affects a monthly payment.

To create a two-variable data table:

1. Enter a formula that contains two input cells.
2. In the same column, below the formula, enter the first list of input values. In the same row, to the right of the formula, enter the second list of input values.
3. Select the range containing both the input values and the formula.
4. In the Data Tools group, click What-If Analysis and choose Data Table to open the Table dialog box.
5. In the Row input cell box, specify the row input cell.
6. In the Column input cell box, specify the column input cell.
7. Click OK.

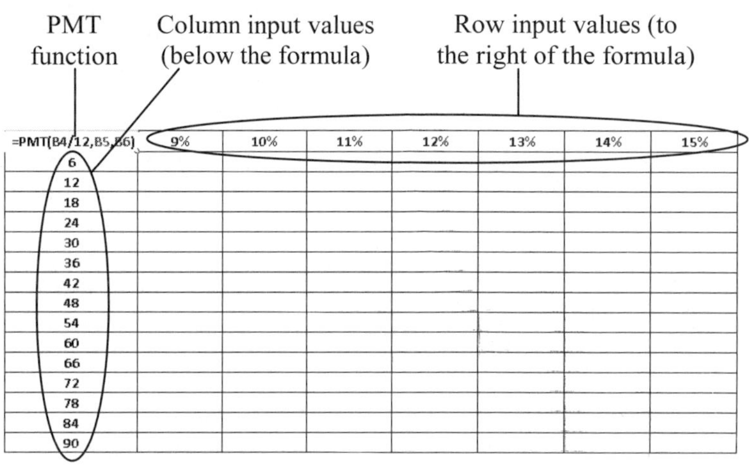

Exhibit 2-3: A two-variable data table

Do it!

C-2: Creating a two-variable data table

Here's how	Here's why
1 Activate the 2v data table sheet	You'll create a two-variable data table to analyze monthly payments.
2 In B7, enter **=PMT(B4/12,B5,B6)**	To calculate monthly payments based on two input cells.
3 Select B7:I22	
Open the Table dialog box	(Click What-If Analysis and choose Data Table.) The insertion point is in the Row input cell box.
4 Select B4	To specify the row input cell.
Place the insertion point in the Column input cell box	
Select B5	To specify the column input cell.
5 Click **OK**	C8:I22 shows how different numbers of months and different interest rates affect the monthly payments for the loan amount in B6.
6 In B6, enter **250000**	The data table now shows payments based on a loan amount of $250,000.
7 Update and close the workbook	

Unit summary: Lookups and data tables

Topic A

In this topic, you learned that lookup functions are used to find a specific value in a worksheet. You used the **VLOOKUP** function to search for a value in a list that is arranged vertically.

Topic B

In this topic, you learned how to use the **MATCH** function to find the relative position of a value in a range. You learned how to use the **INDEX** function to find a value in a range by specifying row and column numbers. You also learned how to use these two functions together to look up information more flexibly than you can with the VLOOKUP function.

Topic C

In this topic, you learned that a **data table** displays the effects of changing the values in a formula. You learned how to use a one-variable data table to observe the effect of changing one variable in a formula. You also learned how to use a two-variable data table to observe the effect of changing two variables in a formula.

Independent practice activity

In this activity, you'll use the VLOOKUP function to search for a value in a list that is arranged vertically. You'll also use the MATCH function, and you'll create a one-variable data table.

1 Open Lookup practice. (Ensure that Lookup is the active worksheet.)

2 Save the workbook as **My lookup practice**.

3 In B6, enter the VLOOKUP function that finds the manager of the city entered in A6. In C6, enter the VLOOKUP function that finds the phone number of the same manager. (*Hint:* The lookup table is named Contact_list. Scroll down to cell A100 to see the correct formulas for B6 and C6.)

4 Activate the Match worksheet. In B6, use the MATCH function to find the number of managers with fewer accounts than the value entered in A6. (*Hint:* The accounts column is named Num_accounts. Scroll down to cell A100 to see the correct formula for B6.)

5 Activate the 1v data table worksheet. In F6:G21, create a one-variable data table to calculate the monthly payments for the various payment schedules in F7:F21. Use the PMT function with an annual interest rate of 10%. Compare your results with Exhibit 2-4. (*Hint:* Scroll down to cell A100 to see the correct formula for G6.)

6 Update and close the workbook.

Payment analysis	
No. of monthly payments	Monthly deduction
See left table	-728.55
6	-2,081.21
12	-1,066.51
18	-728.55
24	-559.78
30	-458.69
36	-391.43
42	-343.51
48	-307.67
54	-279.89
60	-257.75
66	-239.70
72	-224.74
78	-212.13
84	-201.39
90	-192.13

Exhibit 2-4: The results obtained after Step 5 of the independent practice activity

Review questions

1 The VLOOKUP function is a vertical lookup function that finds values in a lookup table that has row labels in the leftmost column. True or false?

2 What is the syntax of the VLOOKUP function?

3 List three important points to remember about the VLOOKUP function.

4 What is the purpose of the MATCH function?

5 What is a data table?

Unit 3

Advanced list management

Unit time: 45 minutes

Complete this unit, and you'll know how to:

A Use the data validation feature to validate data entered in cells.

B Use database functions to summarize list values that meet the criteria you specify.

Topic A: Validating cell entries

This topic covers the following Microsoft Certified Application Specialist exam objective for Excel 2007.

#	Objective

1.2.1	**Restrict data by using data validation**
	• Restrict the type of data that can be entered in cells
	  • Only numbers less than *x* can be entered
	  • Only data of a specified character length to be entered
	• Restrict the values entered in cells
	• Create drop-down lists

Validating data

You use Excel's data validation feature to ensure that selected cells accept only valid data, such as dates or whole numbers. You can also ensure that users select only valid values from a list.

Validating data ensures that data entries match a specified format. You can display a message that prompts users for correct entries or responds to incorrect entries.

You can also specify that Excel should automatically display a circle around invalid entries. To do this, add the Circle Invalid Data button to the Quick Access toolbar.

Do it!

A-1: Observing data validation

Here's how	Here's why
1 Open List management	The Observing data validation sheet is active. You'll observe the cells in which only certain kinds of data can be entered.
2 Save the workbook as **My list management**	
3 Verify that the Observing data validation sheet is active	
4 Select B7, as shown	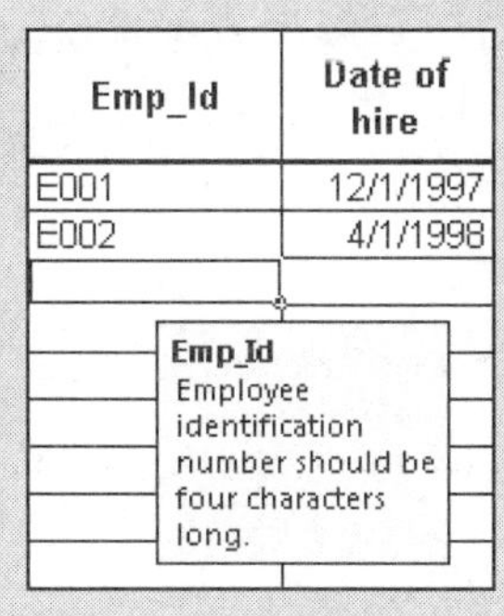 A message appears, stating the acceptable format for Emp_Id numbers.
Enter **E1234**	The Invalid Emp_Id message box appears.

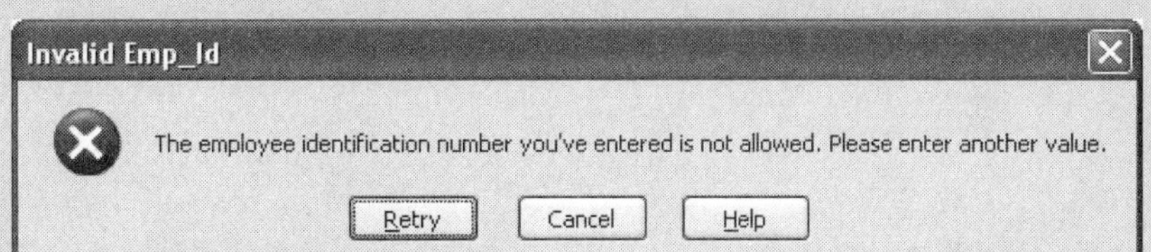

Here's how	Here's why
5 Click **Retry**	To close the message box.
Edit B7 to read **E003**	
Press TAB	The cell accepts the corrected Emp_Id.
6 In C7, enter tomorrow's date	(In mm/dd/yy format.) This date is not permitted because the date-of-hire value cannot be greater than today's date value. The "Invalid date of hire" message box appears.
Click **Cancel**	
7 Enter today's date	The cell accepts the corrected date.

8	Select D7	A drop-down arrow appears to the right of the cell because the cell's validation was set up with a list of possible entries.
	Enter **Sales**	An error message appears.
	Click **Cancel**	To close the message box and clear the cell contents.
9	Click the drop-down arrow	To display the list of valid departments.
	Select **National sales**	
10	Update the workbook	

Setting data validation rules

Explanation

To create a set of rules for data validation:

1. Select the cells for which you want to create a validation rule.
2. On the Data tab, in the Data Tools group, click Data Validation to open the Data Validation dialog box, shown in Exhibit 3-1.
3. Activate the Settings tab.
4. From the Allow list, select a data validation option.
5. From the Data list, select the operator you want to use. Then complete the remaining entries.
6. Click OK to set the validation rule and close the dialog box.

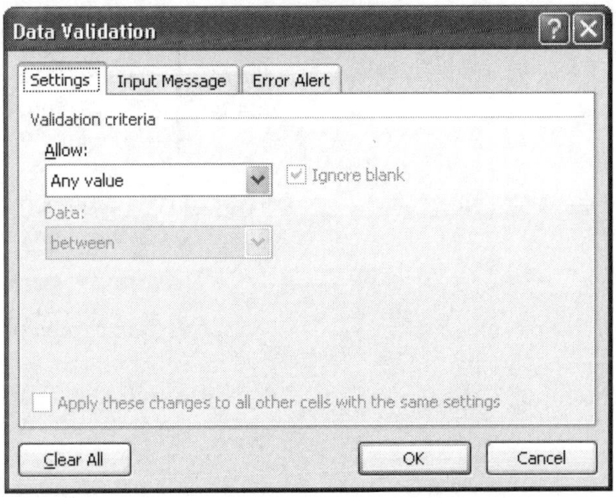

Exhibit 3-1: The Data Validation dialog box

Do it!

A-2: Setting up data validation

Here's how	Here's why
1 Activate the Setting up data validation sheet	
2 Select B5:B20	You'll create a validation rule to ensure that employee numbers are four characters long.
In the Data Tools group, click **Data Validation**	(On the Data tab.) To open the Data Validation dialog box, shown in Exhibit 3-1. By default, the Settings tab is active.
From the Allow list, select **Text length**	To specify the number of characters permitted in each cell of the selected range. The Data list and the Minimum and Maximum boxes appear in the dialog box. The Ignore blank option also becomes available.
From the Data list, select **equal to**	To specify the comparison operator. The Length box replaces the Minimum and Maximum boxes.
In the Length box, enter **4**	To specify the number of characters permitted.
3 Activate the Input Message tab	You'll specify the input message that will appear when the user enters an invalid Emp_Id.
In the Title box, enter **Emp_Id**	This text will appear as a title in the input message.
In the Input message box, enter **Employee identification number should be four characters long.**	This message will appear when the user selects a cell.
4 Activate the Error Alert tab	
In the Title box, enter **Invalid Emp_Id**	This will be the title of the error message box.
In the Error message box, enter **The employee identification number you've entered is not permitted. Please enter another value.**	This is the error message that'll appear when the user enters an invalid employee identification number.
Click **OK**	To set the validation rule.
5 Observe the screen	The input message appears.
6 Select **B5**	

7	Enter **103**	The Invalid Emp_Id message box appears because you entered only three characters.
	Click **Retry**	Or press Enter.
	Enter **E103**	
8	Select C5:C20	You'll create a validation rule to ensure that the date of hire is on or before today's date.
	Open the Data Validation dialog box	Click Data Validation in the Data Tools group on the Data tab.
9	Activate the Settings tab	
	From the Allow list, select **Date**	
	From the Data list, select **less than or equal to**	
	In the End date box, enter **=TODAY()**	To specify the validation date as today's date.
	Click **OK**	To set the validation.
10	In C5, enter tomorrow's date	(In mm/dd/yy format.) An error message appears.
	Click **Retry**	Or press Enter.
	Enter a valid date of hire	A date less than or equal to today's date.
11	Select D5:D20	You'll create a list of valid departments from which the user can choose.
	Open the Data Validation dialog box	The Settings tab is active.
	From the Allow list, select **List**	
	In the Source box, enter **Accounting, Customer support, Human resources, Marketing, National sales**	To create the list of values for the column.
	Click **OK**	To set the validation rule. A drop-down arrow appears to the right of D5.
12	Click the drop-down arrow	
	Select **Marketing**	
13	Update the workbook	

Topic B: Exploring database functions

Explanation

A *database* is an organized collection of related information. In a database, the rows of related data are called *records*, and the columns are called *fields*. The first row of a database contains the names of the fields. In Excel, the terms "database" and "list" mean the same thing.

You can summarize values that meet complex criteria by using database functions, such as DSUM, DCOUNT, and DAVERAGE. For example, you can use DCOUNT to find the total number of salespeople who joined the staff of a specific store in a certain year.

Structure of database functions

The syntax of a database function is:

```
Dfunction(database,field,criteria)
```

In this syntax, the arguments are:

- `database` — The range containing the list of related information. Each row is a record, and each column is a field. The first row of the database must contain labels for each field.
- `field` — The column to be used by the function. Here you can specify the column name, such as Emp_Id, or a number that represents the position of the column in the database.
- `criteria` — The range that contains the conditions a row must meet to be included in the calculation. The function considers only those database records that meet the specified conditions. The first row of the criteria range must include field names that correspond precisely to field names in the database.

  When you include more than one row in the criteria range, the new row is considered to be an "Or" condition. That is, rows will be included if they match the conditions in the first row or if they match conditions in subsequent rows. An Or condition will increase the number of matching rows.

The following examples are based on the database shown in Exhibit 3-2:

- `DSUM(database,"Current year",A2:B3)` returns the total sales of Annatto Seed in the East region for the current year.
- `DCOUNT(database,"Store code",A2:C3)` returns the number of stores in the East region where total sales of Annatto Seed were less than $50,000 for the current year.
- `DSUM(database,"Current year",A2:A4)` returns the total sales of Annatto Seed and Anise Seeds for the current year.

	A	B	C	D	E
1	**Criteria**				
2	**Product**	**Region**	**Current year**		
3	Annatto Seed	East	<50,000		
4	Anise Seeds	North			
5					
6	**Average current year sales of Annatto Seed in East**				$30,479.90
7	**Total current year sales of Annatto Seed and Anise Seeds**				$623,570.92
8	**Number of East region stores where current year total sales of Annatto Seed is less than $50,000**				4
9					
10					
11	**Database**				
12	**Product**	**Region**	**Store code**	**Prior year**	**Current year**
13	Annatto Seed	East	ES008		$24,181.04
14	Cinnamon	East	ES008	$87,970.00	$67,240.00
15	Anise Seeds	East	ES211	$11,312.31	$20,218.31
16	Annatto Seed	East	ES211	$58,842.00	$49,530.00
17	Cinnamon	East	ES211	$99,665.00	$31,705.00
18	Anise Seeds	East	ES367	$22,772.00	$57,510.00
19	Annatto Seed	East	ES367	$17,990.07	$18,157.57
20	Asafoetida Powder	East	ES367	$19,425.69	$23,273.19
21	Cinnamon	East	ES367	$27,517.00	$49,425.00

Exhibit 3-2: A database function worksheet

Do it!

B-1: Examining the structure of database functions

Here's how	Here's why
1 Activate the Database functions sheet	You'll examine the structure of database functions. The blank cells in the Prior year column indicate that this product was not sold by the specific store last year.
Select the range named **Database**	(Select Database from the Name box.) The first row in the range contains unique text labels or field names that identify the data in the columns below them.
Select the range named **Criteria**	This range specifies the conditions for the database functions. The first row contains field names that must exactly match those in the database.
2 Select E6	
Observe the formula bar	fx =DAVERAGE(Database,"Current year",A2:B3) This function calculates the average sales of Annatto Seed in the East region for the current year. In this formula, "Database" is the name of the range that forms the database, "Current year" indicates the column to be used in the function, and "A2:B3" is the criteria range.
3 Select E7	
Observe the formula bar	fx =DSUM(Database,5,A2:A4) This function sums the sales of Annatto Seed and Anise Seeds for the current year. In this formula, "5" represents the column on which the function will perform the calculation. You can use the column number or column name as this argument.
4 Select E8	fx =DCOUNT(Database,"Current year",A2:C3) This function counts the number of stores whose total sales for the current year were less than $50,000 in the East region.

The DSUM and DAVERAGE functions

Explanation

You can use the DSUM function to add only those values in a database column that meet a specified criterion. For example, you could use DSUM to calculate the total sales for a store in a specific year or for one product in a certain region. The syntax of DSUM is:

```
DSUM(database,field,criteria)
```

You can use the DAVERAGE function to average the values in a column of a list or database that match conditions you specify. The syntax of DAVERAGE is:

```
DAVERAGE(database,field,criteria)
```

Do it!

B-2: Using the DSUM function

Here's how	Here's why
1 Activate the DSUM sheet	
Select the range named **Database**	This range forms the database.
2 Select D5	You'll calculate the total sales of Annatto Seed and Anise Seeds of grade A quality.
Type **=DSUM(Database,**	In this formula, "Database" is the name of the range that represents the database.
Type **"Sales",**	This indicates the column on which the function will perform the calculation.
Type **A1:B3)**	"A1:B3" specifies the criteria range.
Press ENTER	The function displays $57,850.35, which is the total sales figure for Annatto Seed and Anise Seeds of grade A quality.
3 Select D6	(If necessary.) You'll sum the values in the Sales column for the Annatto Seed records where the quality grades are B, C, and D.
Type **=DSUM(Database,"Sales",**	
Type **D1:F2)**	The criterion specifies rows in which the grade is both "greater than" A and "less than" E. For letters, this means that the grade characters fall between A and E, in alphabetical order.
Press ENTER	The function displays $139,843.45, which is the total sales figure for Annatto Seed of grades B, C, and D.
4 Update and close the workbook	

Unit summary: Advanced list management

Topic A

In this topic, you learned about the **data validation** feature of Excel. You learned that data validation ensures the entry of valid information in a worksheet. You learned how to specify a set of rules to validate data. You also learned that the validation rules display error messages to prompt the user to enter correct data.

Topic B

In this topic, you learned about **database functions**, such as DSUM, DAVERAGE, and DCOUNT. You learned that database functions are used to summarize data according to specified criteria. You also learned how to use the **DSUM** function to add values that meet complex criteria.

Independent practice activity

In this activity, you'll perform calculations by using several Excel functions. You'll also create data validation rules, and you'll use the DCOUNT function.

1 Open List management practice, and ensure that the Data validation worksheet is active.

2 Save the workbook as **My list management practice**.

3 Create a data validation rule to accept only those Store codes with lengths between four and six characters in the range A5:A24. (*Hint:* Data Validation is in the Data Tools group on the Data tab.)

4 Create a list of regions from which users can choose for the range B5:B24. The list should contain **East**, **North**, **South**, and **West**. Also, ensure that a proper error message appears when the user enters an invalid region.

5 Create a data validation rule to ensure that the range C5:C24 accepts only whole numbers greater than zero.

6 Activate the Database functions worksheet. In H5, enter a database function that counts the number of salespeople whose total sales were greater than $10,000 and whose sales in quarter 3 were greater than $3,000. (*Hint:* Use the DCOUNT function. Your answer should be 4. If you need help with the formula, scroll down to A100.)

7 Update and close the workbook.

Review questions

1 What's the purpose of validating data?

2 List the steps you would use to set data validation rules.

3 In Excel, what is the difference between the terms "database" and "list?"

4 What is the syntax of the DSUM function?

Unit 4

PivotTables and PivotCharts

Unit time: 50 minutes

Complete this unit, and you'll know how to:

A Use the PivotTable command to create a PivotTable for analyzing and comparing large amounts of data.

B Change PivotTable views by moving fields and hiding and showing details.

C Improve the appearance of a PivotTable by applying a style and changing its field settings.

D Create a PivotChart to graphically display data from a PivotTable.

Topic A: Working with PivotTables

Explanation

By analyzing data, you can make more informed decisions. Excel provides the PivotTable feature to help you examine data. A *PivotTable* is an interactive table that summarizes, organizes, and compares large amounts of data in a worksheet. You can rotate the rows and columns in a PivotTable to obtain different views of the same data. You can use a PivotTable to analyze data in an Excel workbook or data from an external database, such as Microsoft Access or SQL Server.

Examining PivotTables

The data on which a PivotTable is based is called the *source data*. Each column represents a *field*, or category of information, which you can assign to different parts of the PivotTable to determine how the data is arranged. You can add four types of fields, shown in Exhibit 4-1 and explained in the following table:

Field	Description
Report Filter	Filters the summarized data in the PivotTable. If you select an item in the report filter, the view of the PivotTable changes to display only the summarized data associated with that item. For example, if Region is a report filter, you can display the summarized data for the North region, the West region, or all regions.
Row Labels	Displays the items in a field as row labels. For example, in Exhibit 4-1, the row labels are values in the Quarter field, which means that the table shows one row for each quarter.
Column Labels	Displays the items in a field as column labels. For example, in Exhibit 4-1, the column labels are values in the Product field, which means that the table shows one column for each product.
Σ Values	Contains the summarized data. These fields usually contain numeric data, such as sales and inventory figures. The area where the data itself appears is called the *data area*.

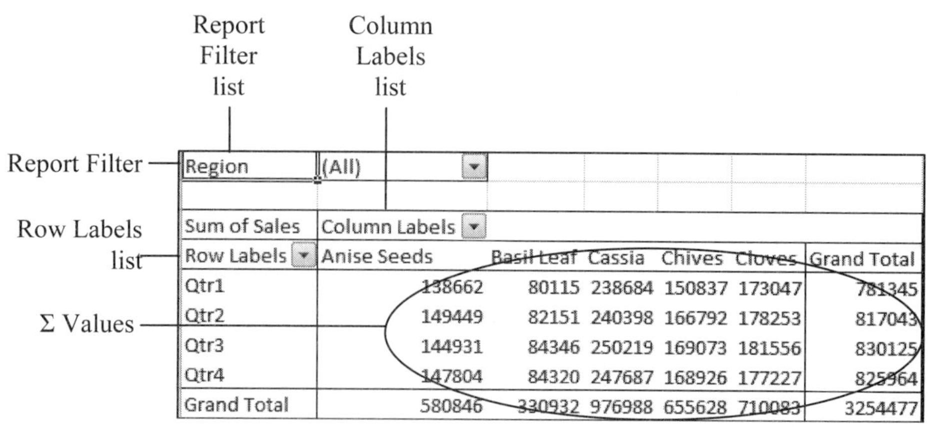

Region	(All)					
Sum of Sales	Column Labels					
Row Labels	Anise Seeds	Basil Leaf	Cassia	Chives	Cloves	Grand Total
Qtr1	138662	80115	238684	150837	173047	781345
Qtr2	149449	82151	240398	166792	178253	817043
Qtr3	144931	84346	250219	169073	181556	830125
Qtr4	147804	84320	247687	168926	177227	825964
Grand Total	580846	330932	976988	655628	710083	3254477

Exhibit 4-1: A sample PivotTable

The PivotTable command

You use the PivotTable command to create a PivotTable. To create a PivotTable:

1. Select any cell in a data range that includes a heading for each column in the top row.
2. Activate the Insert tab.
3. In the Tables group, click the PivotTable button to open the Create PivotTable dialog box. (Or click the PivotTable button's down-arrow and choose PivotTable.)
4. In the Table/Range box, select the range that contains the data to be used in the PivotTable.
5. Select a location for the PivotTable. You can place the PivotTable in a new or existing worksheet.
6. Click OK.

When you insert or work with PivotTables, Excel displays the PivotTable Tools, adding Options and Design tabs to the Ribbon.

Do it!

A-1: Creating a PivotTable

Here's how	Here's why
1 Open PivotTable	(From the current unit folder.) The Raw Data worksheet contains the sales details for several products. You'll use the data in this worksheet to create a PivotTable.
2 Save the workbook as **My PivotTable**	In the current unit folder.
3 Select any cell in the range A5:D105	You'll create a PivotTable based on this range. If you select a cell within the range of the source data, you don't have to specify the range later.
4 Activate the Insert tab	
5 In the Tables group, click the PivotTable button	 To open the Create PivotTable dialog box. It prompts you to select the location of the data you want to analyze. You can use an external data source or an Excel worksheet. The default is the range it determines automatically from the selected cell. In this dialog box, you also specify the location of the PivotTable report. You can create the PivotTable in a new or existing worksheet. The default selection is New worksheet.
Click **OK**	A new worksheet, Sheet1, is added to the workbook. This worksheet displays the layout of the PivotTable; the PivotTable Field List task pane appears; and the PivotTable Tools | Options and Design tabs appear on the Ribbon.
6 Edit the Sheet1 tab name to read **PivotTable**	Double-click the name, type the new one, and press Enter.
7 Update the workbook	

Add fields

Explanation

You can add fields to a PivotTable to specify the data you want to display. The fields of the source data appear in the PivotTable Field List task pane.

To add fields, drag a relevant field from the top of the PivotTable Field List to one of the four areas at the bottom of the task pane. You can add more than one field to an area, and you don't need to add all fields to the table. To display data and not just headings, you need to place at least one field in the Σ Values area.

After the fields are in place, you can filter the information that appears in the table by selecting options from the Filter columns, Filter rows, or Report Filter lists. For example, you can show all data values, or restrict the PivotTable to summarizing only a couple of values.

Do it!

A-2: Adding fields to a PivotTable

Here's how	Here's why
1 Verify that the PivotTable sheet is active	You'll add fields in the PivotTable layout.
Observe the PivotTable Field List task pane	It displays the column headings of the source data in the PivotTable worksheet.
2 Point to **Region**	The pointer turns into a four-headed arrow. You'll use Region as a report filter.
Drag **Region** to Report Filter, as shown	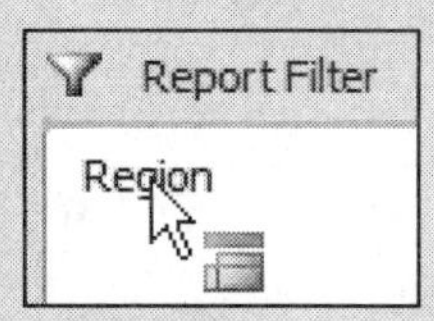 (In the task pane.) In the worksheet, Region appears in cell A1 with a drop-down arrow.
3 Drag **Quarter** to Row Labels	To add Quarter as a row field in the PivotTable.
4 Drag **Product** to Column Labels	To add Product as a column field.
5 Drag **Sales** to Σ Values	To add Sales as the Values item. The PivotTable shows the sum of the quarterly sales for several products. You can change the view by changing the selections in the Filter Column, Filter Rows, and Region lists.

6 In the worksheet, click as shown

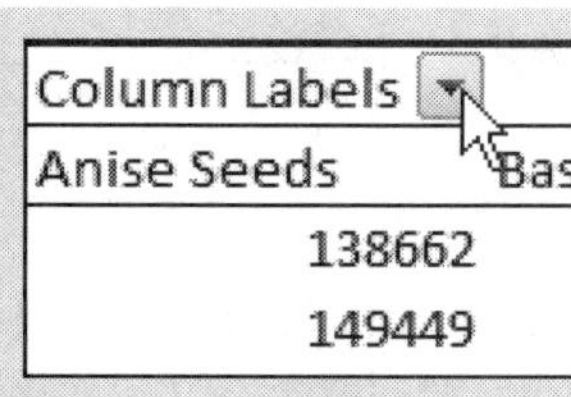

To display a drop-down menu that includes a Product list.

Clear **Basil Leaf**, **Cassia**, and **Cloves**

To specify that the only products shown will be Anise Seeds and Chives.

Click **OK**

The worksheet now shows the sales figures for only Anise Seeds and Chives.

7 Click as shown

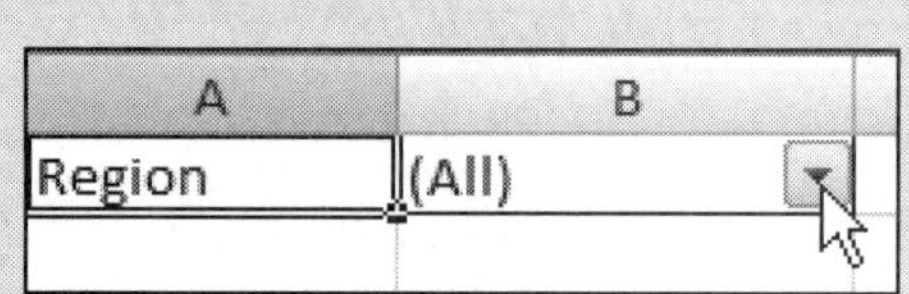

To display the Region list.

From the Region list, select **Central**

To specify that the view will include the sales of Anise Seeds and Chives in the Central region only.

Click **OK**

To close the list. The PivotTable displays the sales of Anise Seeds and Chives in the Central region.

8 In the Filter Columns list, select **Clear Filter from "Product"**

To display data for all of the products.

Display data for all of the products for all regions

In the Region list, select (All).

9 Update the workbook

Topic B: Rearranging PivotTables

Explanation

After creating a PivotTable, you might want to display an entirely different view of the data. You can change the data view by dragging the fields to other areas in the PivotTable. The PivotTable provides options to show or hide the details. To change data in the PivotTable, however, you need to refresh the table after changing the source data.

Move fields

You can move a field in a PivotTable by dragging the field to a new area in the PivotTable Field List task pane. To show a columnar view of the data, as shown in Exhibit 4-2, drag a report or row field to the Column Labels box in the task pane. When you want to arrange data in row fields, drag a report or column field to the Row Labels box in the task pane.

Sum of Sales	Column Labels				
Row Labels	Qtr1	Qtr2	Qtr3	Qtr4	Grand Total
⊟Anise Seeds	138662	149449	144931	147804	580846
Central	26000	33112	28874	27220	115206
East	25617	27818	28224	31321	112980
North	29269	29919	28433	27363	114984
South	12776	12600	12900	13400	51676
West	45000	46000	46500	48500	186000
⊟Basil Leaf	80115	82151	84346	84320	330932
Central	13800	15080	12821	16363	58064
East	18213	17849	18291	15345	69698
North	16955	15532	17834	16710	67031
South	15435	17345	18200	16982	67962
West	15712	16345	17200	18920	68177
⊟Cassia	238684	240398	250219	247687	976988

Exhibit 4-2: A PivotTable

Do it!

B-1: Moving fields

Here's how	Here's why
1 Observe the PivotTable	It shows the quarterly sales of several products. You'll move the fields to show the data in a different way.
2 In the PivotTable Field List task pane, drag **Product** below Quarter	The list of products appears beneath each quarter name in the PivotTable.
3 Drag **Quarter** to Column Labels	(In the task pane.) Each quarter appears in a column in the PivotTable.
	You'll change Region from a report filter to a row label.
4 Drag **Region** above Product, as shown	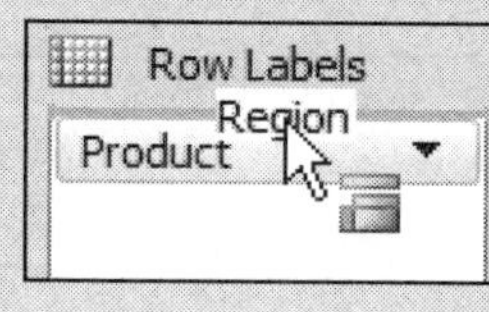
	To change Region from a report filter to a row label, making the list of products appear indented beneath each region name in the PivotTable.
	The order of the fields in the Row Labels list affects the structure of the PivotTable.
5 Drag **Region** below Product	
6 Observe the PivotTable	The regions and products switch hierarchical order in the spreadsheet, with regions now appearing indented beneath products, as shown in Exhibit 4-2.
7 Update the workbook	

Collapse and expand details

Explanation

You can collapse and expand details in a PivotTable that has more than one row or column field. This can help you summarize the data more concisely.

To hide details:

1. Select the cell or range you want to collapse.
2. Activate the PivotTable Tools | Options tab.
3. In the Active Field group, click Collapse Entire Field.

To expand a collapsed range, select it and click Expand Entire Field in the Active Field group on the PivotTable Tools | Options tab.

Do it!

B-2: Hiding and showing details

Here's how	Here's why
1 In the PivotTable Field List pane, under Row Labels, drag **Region** above Product	
Select A5:F34	You'll hide the sales details for products and show only the total sales for each region.
2 On the Ribbon, activate the PivotTable Tools | Options tab	If necessary.
3 In the Active Field group, click as shown	

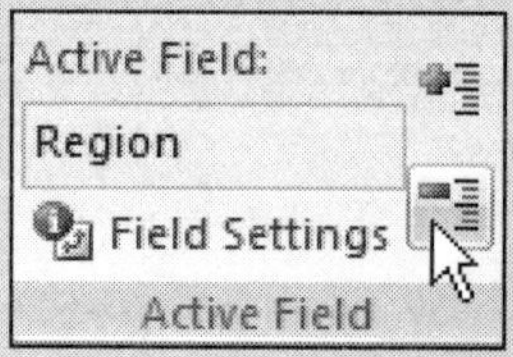

To hide the product sales details.

Deselect the range

Sum of Sales	Column Labels				
Row Labels	Qtr1	Qtr2	Qtr3	Qtr4	Grand Total
⊞Central	123443	141209	139751	134895	539298
⊞East	149506	151044	154530	160748	615828
⊞North	168402	171468	169938	162776	672584
⊞South	156152	161980	165738	166260	650130
⊞West	183842	191342	200168	201285	776637
Grand Total	781345	817043	830125	825964	3254477

The worksheet shows only a summary of the sales details for each region.

4 Click as shown

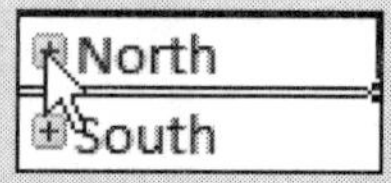

To reveal the product details for the North region. Next, you'll show all of the details for all regions.

5 Select A5:F14

6 On the Options tab, in the Active Field group, click as shown

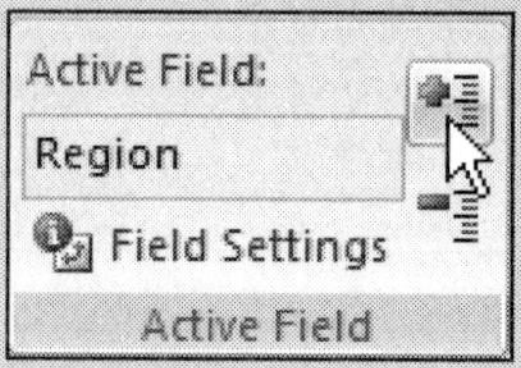

To show the regional sales details for each product.

7 Update the workbook

Refresh data

Explanation

You cannot directly change the data in a PivotTable because it's based on source data.

To change data in a PivotTable, you must first change the source data and then refresh the PivotTable to reflect the latest changes. You can refresh the PivotTable by clicking the Refresh button in the Data group on the Options tab.

Do it!

B-3: Refreshing the data in a PivotTable

Here's how	Here's why
1 Select B18	It shows the value 29269.
Enter **30000**	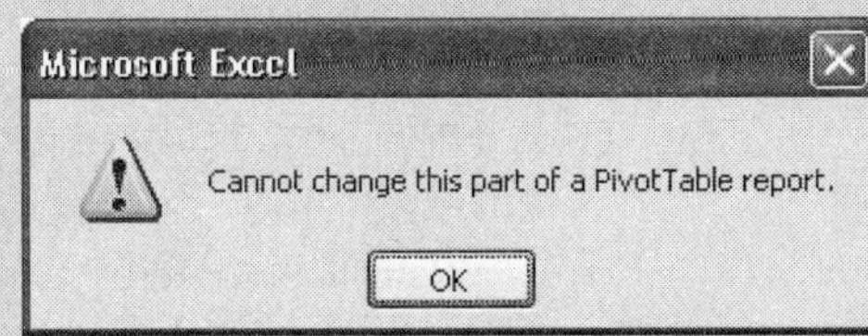 When you try to enter the first character, a message box appears with a warning that you can't change the value in a PivotTable.
Click **OK**	To close the message box.
2 Activate the Raw Data sheet	This contains the source data for the PivotTable. To change the data in the PivotTable, you have to change the values in the worksheet.
3 Select D46	The cell shows the value $29,269. You'll change this value and then view the result in the PivotTable.
Edit D46 to read **30000**	This cell is the only contributor to the value of B6 in the PivotTable.
4 Activate the PivotTable sheet	Notice that B18 still shows the old value.
5 Activate the Options tab	If necessary.
6 In the Data group, click the Refresh button	 (Click the icon in the top half of the button.) To update the PivotTable with the latest data. B18 now shows the new value.
7 Update the workbook	

Topic C: Formatting PivotTables

Explanation

You can change the format of a PivotTable by using styles and the Field Settings dialog box. You can use styles to format an entire PivotTable in one step. You can use the Field Settings dialog box to change number formats, specify how data is summarized, and show or hide data.

Use styles

To display formatting options that affect the entire PivotTable, activate the PivotTable Tools | Design tab. Some of the styles are specifically designed for PivotTables. Exhibit 4-3 shows a sample Pivot style.

Sum of Sales	Column Labels			
Row Labels	Qtr1	Qtr2	Qtr3	Qtr4	Grand Total
Central	123443	141209	139751	134895	539298
Anise Seeds	26000	33112	28874	27220	115206
Basil Leaf	13800	15080	12821	16363	58064
Cassia	45000	43983	46343	45892	181218
Chives	18300	25034	28679	25655	97668
Cloves	20343	24000	23034	19765	87142
East	149506	151044	154530	160748	615828
Anise Seeds	25617	27818	28224	31321	112980
Basil Leaf	18213	17849	18291	15345	69698
Cassia	44353	43245	42834	41853	172285
Chives	33645	36454	34745	36564	141408
Cloves	27678	25678	30436	35665	119457

Exhibit 4-3: A sample Pivot style

Do it!

C-1: Formatting by using a Pivot style

Here's how	Here's why
1 Activate the Design tab	Under PivotTable Tools, on the Ribbon.
2 In the PivotTable Styles group, click as shown	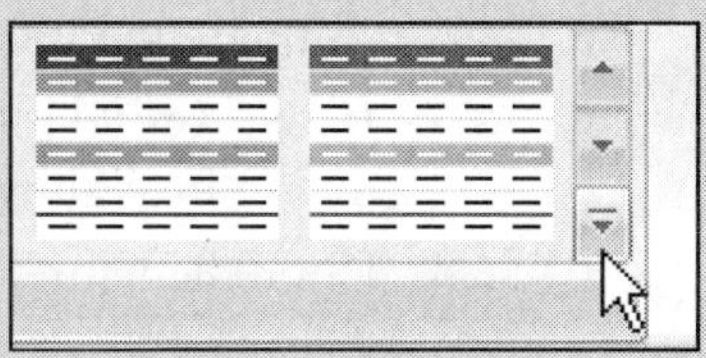 To open the PivotTable Styles gallery.
3 Under Medium, click as shown	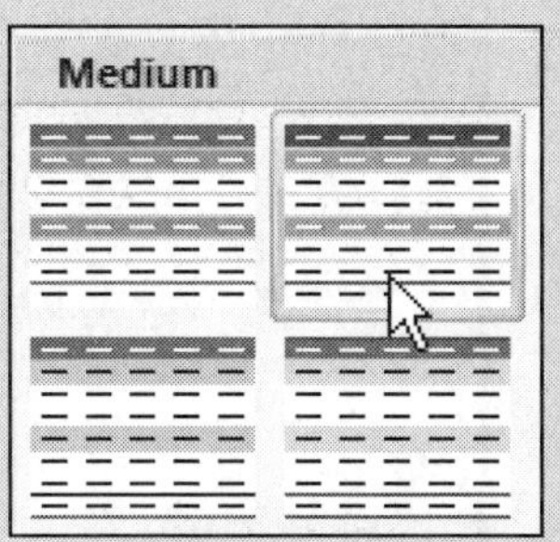 To apply Pivot Style Medium 2 to the PivotTable. The PivotTable appears as shown in Exhibit 4-3.
4 Update the workbook	

Change field settings

Explanation

You can change field settings to alter how data appears or is summarized in a PivotTable. To change field settings:

1. Select any cell in the data area.
2. Activate the PivotTable Tools | Options tab.
3. In the Active Field group, click Field Settings to open the Value Field Settings dialog box, shown in Exhibit 4-4.
4. Click the Number Format button to open the Format Cells dialog box. Select the desired options and click OK.
5. Click OK.

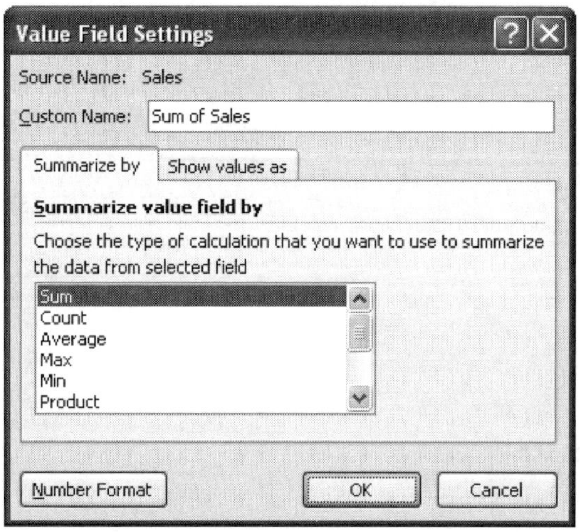

Exhibit 4-4: The Value Field Settings dialog box

Do it!

C-2: Changing field settings

Here's how	Here's why
1 Select B18	(If necessary.) This cell is in the data area. You'll apply a number format to the data items.
2 Activate the Options tab	
3 In the Active Field group, click **Field Settings**	To open the Value Field Settings dialog box, shown in Exhibit 4-4.
4 Click **Number Format**	To open the Format Cells dialog box.
From the Category list, sclect **Number**	
Check **Use 1000 Separator (,)**	To display a comma after the thousands place in the number.
5 From the Category list, select **Currency**	To display the formatting options under Currency. The $ option is selected in the Symbol list. You'll add this prefix symbol to the sales values.
Edit the Decimal places box to read **0**	To specify that currency values should be displayed as whole-dollar amounts.
6 Click **OK**	To close the Format Cells dialog box.
Click **OK**	To close the Value Field Settings dialog box and apply the formatting to all Sales field values (not just the selected cell). The values are now formatted with commas and the $ symbol.
7 Update the workbook	

Topic D: PivotCharts

Explanation

You can use a PivotChart to graphically display data from a PivotTable. A single PivotChart provides different views of the same data.

Create PivotCharts

When you create a PivotChart, the row fields of the PivotTable become the categories, and the column fields become the series.

To create a PivotChart, select any cell in a PivotTable and click PivotChart in the Tools group on the Options tab. In the Insert Chart dialog box, select options as you would for a standard chart, and then click OK.

You can also create a new PivotChart and PivotTable at the same time. To do so, you select a cell in the source data, activate the Insert tab, click the PivotTable button's down-arrow (in the Tables group), and choose PivotChart.

Do it!

D-1: Creating a PivotChart

Here's how	Here's why
1 Click anywhere within the PivotTable	(If necessary.) To indicate which data to use for the PivotChart.
2 Activate the Options tab	If necessary.
In the Tools group, click **PivotChart**	To open the Insert Chart dialog box. You'll create the default Column chart.
Click **OK**	To create a PivotChart in a floating box on this sheet. The PivotChart Filter Pane appears, showing the active fields on the PivotChart. The chart's x-axis displays the Row Labels fields; the legend displays the Column labels fields; and the bars represents the data values. You'll change the PivotTable and chart to show only the total sales for each region.
3 In the PivotTable Field List pane, drag **Product** to Report Filter	To make Product a report filter. You can now sort and filter data in the PivotChart by using Product.
Observe the PivotChart	The total sales for the five regions appear in columns, and each column is divided into quarters. You can use the Product, Region, and Quarter lists to change the data represented by the PivotChart.
Resize and move the chart so it no longer overlaps the table	(If necessary.) Drag the chart box's edges and corners as necessary.
4 From the Product list, select **Basil Leaf**	The Product list is located in B1.
Click **OK**	The PivotChart displays the total sales of only Basil Leaf for all regions.
5 In the Column Labels list, clear all of the options except Qtr1	
Click **OK**	The chart displays the total sales of Basil Leaf in the first quarter for all regions.
6 Update and close the workbook	

Unit summary: PivotTables and PivotCharts

Topic A In this topic, you learned that a **PivotTable** is used to summarize, organize, and compare large amounts of data in a worksheet. You learned how to create a PivotTable and how to add fields to the layout of a PivotTable.

Topic B In this topic, you learned how to change the appearance of data in a PivotTable by moving the **row** and **column fields** to different areas. You also learned how to **hide** and **show details** in the PivotTable.

Topic C In this topic, you learned how to apply **styles** to format an entire PivotTable. You also learned how to use the Value Field Settings dialog box to apply formatting to numerical data.

Topic D In this topic, you learned that a **PivotChart** graphically displays data from a PivotTable. You also learned how to create a PivotChart. You learned that moving the fields in the PivotChart changes the way data is presented.

Independent practice activity

In this activity, you'll create a PivotTable. You'll also modify a PivotTable and apply a style to it. Finally, you'll create and modify a PivotChart.

1. Open PivotTable practice.
2. Save the workbook as **My PivotTable practice**.
3. Create a PivotTable based on the data in the Raw Data worksheet. (*Hint:* Select within the data, and click the PivotTable button on the Insert tab.)
4. Move Year to the Row Labels area, move Quarter to the Column Labels area, move Product to the Row Labels area below the Year field, and move Sales to the Σ Values area. Compare your results with Exhibit 4-5.
5. Apply the Pivot Style Medium 3 to the PivotTable.
6. Create a basic column PivotChart. (*Hint:* Activate the Options tab.)
7. Make Quarter and Year report filters in the PivotChart. (*Hint:* Drag the fields to Report Filters.)
8. Compare your results with Exhibit 4-6.
9. Change the PivotChart to display the sales in the fourth quarter of 2006.
10. Update and close the workbook.

Sum of Sales	Column Labels				
Row Labels	Qtr1	Qtr2	Qtr3	Qtr4	Grand Total
⊟2002	123443	141209	139751	134895	539298
Anise Seeds	26000	33112	28874	27220	115206
Basil Leaf	13800	15080	12821	16363	58064
Cassia	45000	43983	46343	45892	181218
Chives	18300	25034	28679	25655	97668
Cloves	20343	24000	23034	19765	87142
⊟2003	139490.59	159566.17	157918.63	152431.35	609406.74
Anise Seeds	29380	37416.56	32627.62	30758.6	130182.78
Basil Leaf	15594	17040.4	14487.73	18490.19	65612.32
Cassia	50850	49700.79	52367.59	51857.96	204776.34
Chives	20679	28288.42	32407.27	28990.15	110364.84
Cloves	22987.59	27120	26028.42	22334.45	98470.46

Exhibit 4-5: The PivotTable after Step 4 of the independent practice activity

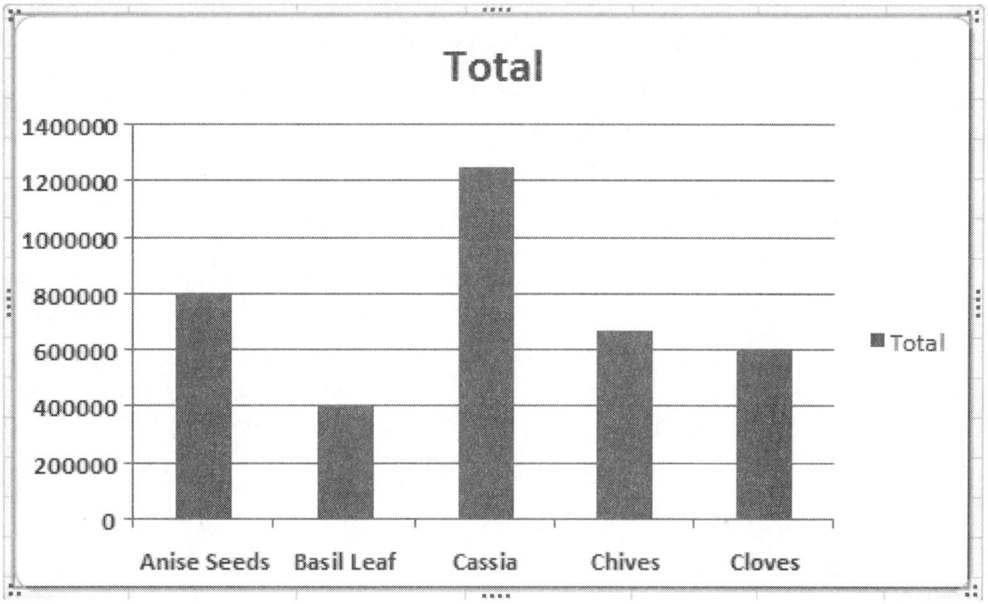

Exhibit 4-6: The PivotChart after Step 8 of the independent practice activity

Review questions

1 What is a PivotTable?

2 How do you start creating a PivotTable?

3 Can you directly change the data in a PivotTable? If not, how do you change the data?

4 Why would you use a PivotChart?

5 How do you create a PivotChart?

Unit 5

Exporting and importing

Unit time: 50 minutes

Complete this unit, and you'll know how to:

A Export data from Excel to a text file, and import data from a text file into an Excel workbook.

B Import XML data into a workbook, and export data from a workbook to an XML data file.

C Use Microsoft Query and the Web query feature to import data from external databases.

Topic A: Exporting and importing text files

This topic covers the following Microsoft Certified Application Specialist exam objectives for Excel 2007.

#	Objective
1.2.2	**Remove duplicate rows from spreadsheets** • Select which columns are used to determine duplication
2.3.5	**Convert text to columns**

Options for importing and exporting

Explanation

You can share information between Excel and other programs in a number of ways, including by using linked objects and copied data. Another way to share data is to export it from Excel to another format or to import data from another format into Excel. Excel can import from and export to files in several formats, including text files.

Use the Save As command to export data

You can use the Save As command to save an Excel workbook in a file format associated with the program in which you want to use the data. However, an Excel workbook that's saved in a different file format might not retain its original formatting.

When you save an Excel workbook in the Text (Tab delimited) file format, the text and values in the cells are saved as they appear in the Excel worksheet. If the cells contain formulas instead of values, however, the formulas are saved as text.

In a text file, tab characters separate the columns of data, and each row of data starts in a new paragraph. In addition, the formatting, graphics, and objects are not saved when you export data to a text file.

Do it!

A-1: Exporting Excel data to a text file

	Here's how	Here's why
1	Open Exporting	From the current unit folder.
2	Open the Save As dialog box	The default name of the file is Exporting.
	From the Save as type list, select **Text (Tab delimited)**	This will save the worksheet as a tab-delimited text file.
	Click **Save**	To save the worksheet as a text file. A message appears, stating that Excel will not save those features that are not compatible with the Text (Tab delimited) file format.
	Click **Yes**	To keep the tab-delimited format.
3	Click **Start**	
	Choose **All Programs**, **Accessories**, **Notepad**	To open the Notepad program.
	Open the Exporting text file	(From the current unit folder.) The data from the Exporting worksheet appears in the text file. All of the sales figures that contain commas appear in double quotation marks.
	Close Notepad	
4	Switch to Excel	If necessary.
5	Close the workbook	You don't need to save changes.

Import data

Explanation

By using the Open command in Excel, you can open a file created in a program other than Excel. After importing the data, you can save the file either in its original format or as an Excel workbook.

To import a file into an Excel workbook, open the Open dialog box, specify the type of file you want to import, select the file, and click Open.

If you're importing a text file, Excel displays the Text Import Wizard, shown in Exhibit 5-1. The wizard guides you through the process of converting the text data into an Excel worksheet. As necessary, you can specify *delimiters* (the characters that determine when a new column should begin) and formatting for specific columns. After importing, you can also separate text into columns, if necessary, by clicking Text to Columns in the Data Tools group on the Data tab.

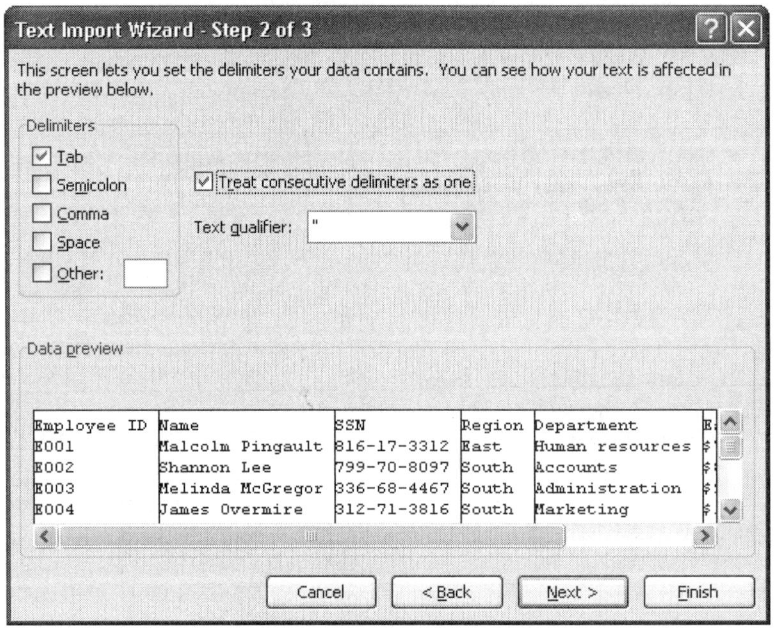

Exhibit 5-1: Step 2 of the Text Import Wizard

Do it!

A-2: Importing data from a text file into a workbook

Here's how	Here's why
1 Start Notepad	Click Start and choose All Programs, Accessories, Notepad.
Open the Employee List text file	You'll import data from this text file into Excel. This file contains details for employees, with columns separated by tab characters.
Observe the date format in the last column	The person who entered this data used the European day/month/year format, not the American month/day/year format.
2 Close Notepad	
3 Switch to Excel	If necessary.
4 Open the Open dialog box	
From the Look in list, select the current unit folder	If necessary.
From the Files of type list, select **Text Files**	To display only the text files in the current unit folder.
Select **Employee list**	To select the file you want to import.
5 Click **Open**	To open Step 1 of the Text Import Wizard. Under Original data type, Delimited is selected. The "Start import at row" box displays "1."
Click **Next**	In Step 2 of the Text Import Wizard, you set the delimiter and see a preview of the data. Here, Tab is the default delimiter.
Under Data preview, observe the box	This box shows you how the data will look in Excel. Data in a few columns is misaligned with the heading because of the consecutive tabs.
Check **Treat consecutive delimiters as one**	To remove the blank columns, as shown in Exhibit 5-1.
6 Click **Next**	In Step 3 of the Text Import Wizard, you can specify the data format for each column.

7	Select the last column	(Scroll to the right as necessary.) You must indicate that the values are currently in DMY (day/month/year) format for Excel to be able to change the formatting to the American MDY format.
	Under Column data format, select **Date**	
	From the Date format list, select **DMY**	
8	Click **Finish**	To close the Text Import Wizard.

	A	B	C	D	E	F	G
1	Employee	Name	SSN	Region	Departme	Earnings	Date of Hire
2	E001	Malcolm F	816-17-33	East	Human re	$73,500	########
3	E002	Shannon L	799-70-80	South	Accounts	$80,000	2/1/2002
4	E003	Melinda N	336-68-44	South	Administr	$95,000	########
5	E004	James Ov	312-71-38	South	Marketing	$105,000	########
6	E005	Roger Wil	534-98-75	East	Customer	$90,000	########
7	E005	Roger Wil	534-98-75	East	Customer	$90,000	########
8	E006	Annie Phi	856-85-85	West	Human re	$60,000	########

The worksheet shows the data from the text file. Some columns are too narrow to display all of the data.

9	Select columns A through G	Drag through the column headings.
	Double-click the dividing line between any two selected column headings	To automatically fit the width to the column contents.
10	Observe the Date of Hire column data	(see below)

Date of Hire
4/19/2001
2/1/2002
7/22/1999
6/14/1997

Excel converted the dates to its standard MDY format.

11	Open the Save As dialog box	The File name box contains "Employee list," and the Save as type list displays Text (Tab delimited).
	From the Save as type list, select **Excel Workbook**	(You might have to scroll up the list to view the option.) To save the data in an Excel workbook.
	Edit the File name box to read **My employee list**	
12	Click **Save**	

Convert text to columns

The Text to Columns feature enables you to divide text fields into two or more columns. This works much like importing data from external text files. For instance, if you have one field for names, you can split this field into first-name and last-name columns. To do so, select the text field you'd like to convert and click Text to Columns on the Data tab. Follow the instructions in the Convert Text to Columns Wizard.

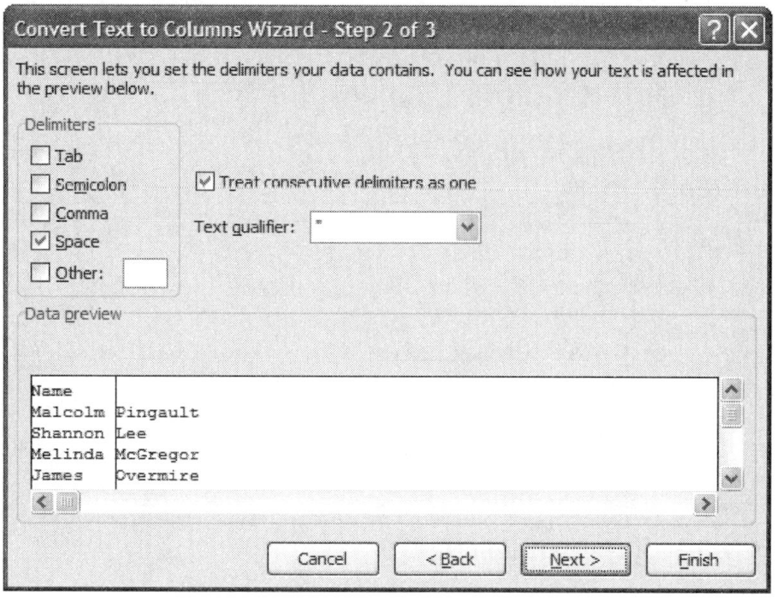

Exhibit 5-2: Step 2 of the Convert Text to Columns Wizard

Do it!

A-3: Converting text to columns

Here's how	Here's why
1 Insert a column after column B	(Select column C, right-click it, and choose Insert.) To make room for the new column.
2 Select column B	This is the Name column in the data you just imported from a text file.
3 On the Data tab, in the Data Tools group, click **Text to Columns**	To start the Convert Text to Columns Wizard. This is like a mini version of the Text Import Wizard.
4 Click **Next**	
5 Under Delimiters, clear **Tab** and check **Space**	
Check **Treat consecutive delimiters as one**	Verify that Treat consecutive delimiters as one is checked.
Click **Next**	To proceed to the last step in the wizard.
6 Verify the General is selected as the column data format	Note that the column heading Name appears in the first-name column. You'll change the heading after the conversion.
7 Click **Finish**	To close the wizard and return to the table. First and last names are now split into two columns. If you hadn't inserted a new column, Excel would have asked if you wanted to replace the existing data.
8 Edit B1 to read **First Name**	
9 In C1, enter **Last Name**	
10 Adjust column widths as necessary	Select columns B and C and then double-click the divider between them.
11 Update the workbook	

Remove duplicates

Sometimes, especially when you import data from one or more external sources, you can end up with duplicate records. Using the Remove Duplicates dialog box, shown in Exhibit 5-3, you can remove duplicate records based on values in one or more fields. For instance, if you imported customer data from several sources because you want to compile e-mail addresses for a mailing, you can remove duplicates based on the e-mail field.

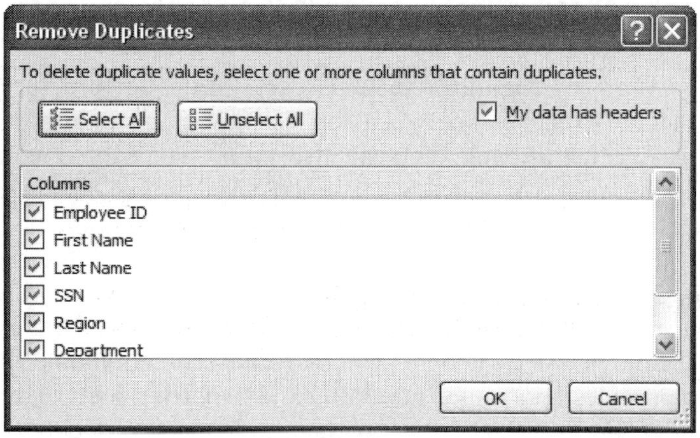

Exhibit 5-3: The Remove Duplicates dialog box

Do it!

A-4: Removing duplicate records

Here's how	Here's why
1 Observe employee numbers E005, E015, and E019	The table has duplicate records.
2 Select the table	 Click the selector in the upper-left corner, as shown.
3 On the Data tab, in the Data Tools group, click **Remove Duplicates**	To open the Remove Duplicates dialog box.
4 Click **Unselect All**	You need to search only one column.
5 Check **SSN**, as shown in Exhibit 5-3	You'll search for duplicates based on the Social Security number, which should be a unique identifier.
6 Click **OK**	To close the Remove Duplicates dialog box. A message box informs you that three duplicates were found and removed.
Click **OK**	To close the message box.
7 Update and close the workbook	

Topic B: Exporting and importing XML data

Explanation

Extensible Markup Language (XML) is a set of rules for structuring and designing data formats that are exchanged between applications. You can import data from an XML file into an Excel workbook. You can also export data from a workbook to an XML file. To import or export XML data, you use the XML Source task pane to map the workbook to a user-defined XML schema (.xsd file).

The XML Source task pane

The XML Source task pane helps you map an Excel workbook to an XML schema. This pane also provides options for importing and exporting XML data. You can also refresh the imported data to reflect the latest changes in the source data.

To map a workbook to a user-defined XML schema:

1. Activate the Developer tab. If it's not visible, enable it:
   a. Click the Office Button and click Excel Options.
   b. Select the Popular category, if necessary, and check "Show Developer tab in the Ribbon."
2. On the Developer tab, in the XML group, click Source to display the XML Source task pane, shown in Exhibit 5-4.
3. In the task pane, click XML Maps to open the XML Maps dialog box, shown in Exhibit 5-5.
4. Click Add to open the Select XML Source dialog box. Browse to locate the .xsd file, and click Open.
5. In the Multiple Roots dialog box that appears, select the .xsd file and click OK.
6. Click OK to close the XML Maps dialog box. The file and the elements in it appear in the XML Source task pane.
7. To map the XML schema to the workbook, drag the elements from the task pane to the corresponding cells in the workbook. The mapped areas appear in blue with nonprintable borders.

Exhibit 5-4: The XML Source task pane

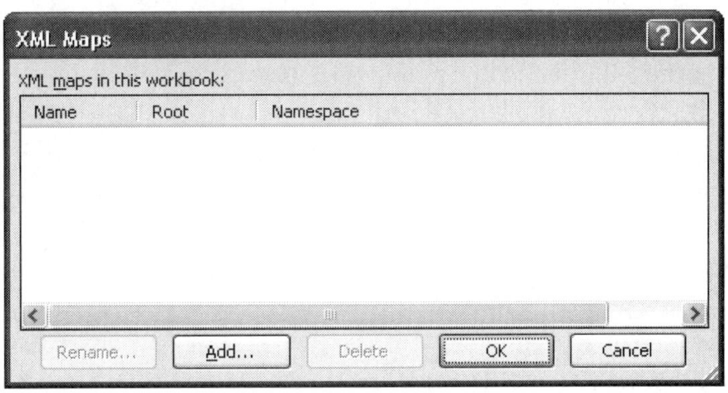

Exhibit 5-5: The XML Maps dialog box

Defining XML options

The XML Source task pane also provides options to display XML data in a worksheet in different formats. Click the Options button in the task pane and choose the option you want. The options are:

- **Preview Data in Task Pane** — Displays data in the XML Source task pane when you import XML data.
- **Hide Help Text in the Task Pane** — Hides the help text that appears below the list of schema elements in the XML Source task pane.
- **Automatically Merge Elements When Mapping** — Expands an XML List automatically when you drag an element from the XML Source task pane to a cell that is outside the XML List but adjacent to it.
- **My Data Has Headings** — Uses existing data as column headings when you create XML maps.

Do it!

B-1: Using the XML Source task pane

Here's how	Here's why
1 Open Employees	(You might need to select Excel Files from the Files of type list in the Open dialog box.) You'll create an XML map for this workbook.
2 Save the workbook as **My employees**	In the current unit folder.
3 Activate the Developer tab	If the Developer tab does not appear, open the Excel Options dialog box, click Popular, check "Show Developer tab in the Ribbon," and click OK.
4 In the XML group, click **Source**	To display the XML Source task pane, shown in Exhibit 5-4.
5 Click **XML Maps**	(In the XML Source task pane.) To open the XML Maps dialog box, shown in Exhibit 5-5.
Click **Add**	To open the Select XML Source dialog box.
From the Look in list, select the current unit folder	If necessary.
Select **EmployeeRecord.xsd**	This is the file containing the XML schema.
Click **Open**	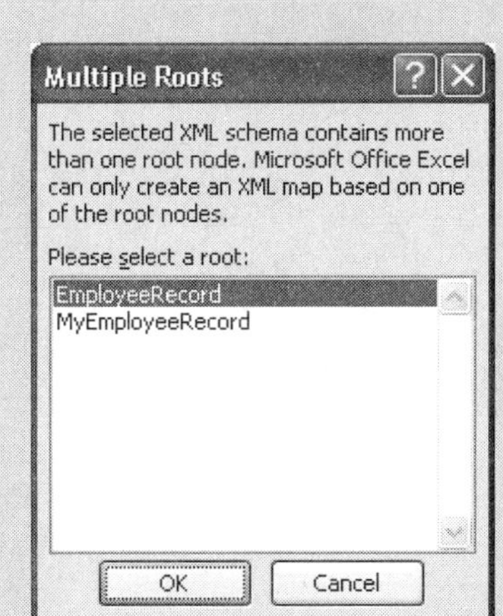 The Multiple Roots dialog box opens with EmployeeRecord selected.
Click **OK**	A message box appears, asking if you want to continue adding this schema to your workbook.
Click **Yes**	

6	Click **OK**	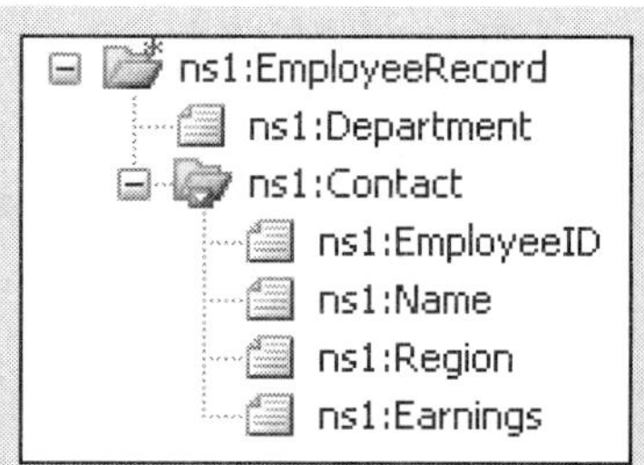 To close the XML Maps dialog box. You can see the .xsd file along with its elements in the XML Source task pane.
7	Drag the note icon that appears to the left of **ns1:Department** from the XML Source task pane to the worksheet, as shown	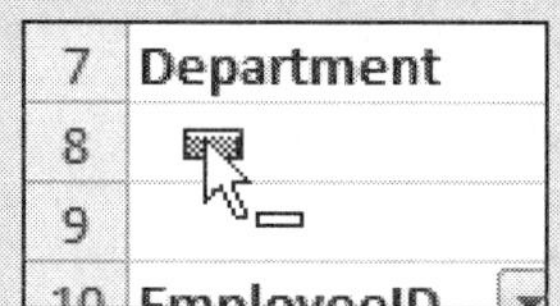 To map the element Department in the XML schema to the worksheet.
	Deselect A8	(Click anywhere in the worksheet.) Now the cell has a blue border, indicating that the cell is mapped to an XML schema.
8	Drag **ns1:EmployeeID** to A11	
	Drag **ns1:Name** to B11	
	Drag **ns1:Region** to C11	
	Drag **ns1:Earnings** to D11	
9	Select E11	To deselect the mapped cells.
10	Update the workbook	

Import XML data into a workbook

Explanation

After creating an XML map, you can import data in an XML format into a workbook. To import XML data:

1. Activate the Developer tab.
2. In the XML group, click Import to open the Import XML dialog box.
3. Select the XML file containing the data. You can use the Look in list to locate the file, if necessary.
4. Click Import. The values in the XML file appear in the corresponding cells in the workbook, as shown in Exhibit 5-6.

Department			
Human resources			
EmployeeID	**Name**	**Region**	**Earnings**
E001	Malcolm Pingault	East	$73,500
E006	Annie Philips	West	$60,000
E011	Paul Anderson	East	$180,000
E019	Jamie Morrison	East	$62,000

Exhibit 5-6: XML data imported into a workbook

Do it!

B-2: Importing XML data into a workbook

Here's how	Here's why
1 In the XML group, click **Import**	(On the Developer tab.) To open the Import XML dialog box.
2 Select **EmployeeInfo**	(From the current unit folder.) This XML file contains values for fields such as Department, EmployeeID, Name, Region, and Earnings in the workbook.
3 Click **Import**	You'll see that the values corresponding to Department, EmployeeID, Name, Region, and Earnings appear in the corresponding cells, as shown in Exhibit 5-6. The Trace Error button appears if you select a value in the Earnings column, because those values are stored as text instead of numbers.
4 Update and close the workbook	

Export data to XML files

Explanation

You can modify the data in a workbook and then export it in XML format so that it can be used by other applications. You can also add or delete records in the workbook.

For you to export data, the workbook should contain a valid XML map. Excel will validate the worksheet data against this map before exporting. To export the workbook data, click Export in the XML group on the Developer tab.

Do it!

B-3: Exporting data from a workbook to an XML data file

Here's how	Here's why
1 Open Export as XML	From the current unit folder.
2 Display the XML Source task pane	(If necessary. To do so, click XML Source in the XML group of the Developer tab.) The workbook is mapped to EmployeeRecord.
3 Save the workbook as **My export as XML**	In the current unit folder.
4 In A21, enter **E038**	To enter the employee ID for someone who has joined the Accounting department.
In B21, enter **David Ford**	
5 In C21, enter **South**	
6 Copy the value in D17	
Paste it in D21	
7 Right-click row heading **16**	(The number 16 at the left of that row.) This row contains the record for an employee who has left the Accounting department.
Choose **Delete**	To delete the record.
8 Update the workbook	
9 Activate the Developer tab	If necessary.
10 In the XML group, click **Export**	To open the Export XML dialog box.
From the Save in list, select the current unit folder	If necessary.
In the File name box, enter **My export as XML**	
11 Click **Export**	To export the workbook as an XML file.

Delete XML maps

Explanation

After importing or exporting data, you no longer need to map the workbook to an XML schema. Therefore, you can delete the XML maps. When you delete a map, the data in the workbook remains.

To delete an XML map:

1. In the XML Source task pane, click XML Maps to open the XML Maps dialog box.
2. Select the XML map you want to delete.
3. Click Delete. A message box appears, warning that you'll no longer be able to import or export XML data by using the XML map. Click OK.
4. Click OK.

Do it!

B-4: Deleting an XML map

Here's how	Here's why
1 In the XML Source task pane, click **XML Maps**	To open the XML Maps dialog box.
2 In the "XML maps in this workbook" list, select the XML map	
Click **Delete**	A message warns you that you'll no longer be able to import or export XML data with this XML map.
Click **OK**	To delete the XML map and close the message box. The XML Maps dialog box no longer displays the XML map.
3 Click **OK**	To close the XML Maps dialog box.
4 Observe the workbook	The data in the workbook remains intact.
5 Update and close the workbook	

Topic C: Querying external databases

Explanation

With Microsoft Query, you can retrieve data from external databases, such as those in Microsoft Access. You can use the Web query feature to retrieve data from the Web.

Microsoft Query

You can use Microsoft Query to retrieve data that meets certain conditions in one or more tables of a database. For example, from an Employee table, you can retrieve the records of all people who work in the Marketing department.

To retrieve data by using Microsoft Query:

1. Activate the Data tab.
2. In the Get External Data group, click From Other Sources and choose From Microsoft Query to start the Microsoft Query program and to open the Choose Data Source dialog box, shown in Exhibit 5-7.
3. On the Databases tab, select <New Data Source> and click OK to open the Create New Data Source dialog box. Specify the name of the data source and select a driver for the database. Click Connect to open the ODBC Microsoft Access Setup dialog box.
4. Under Database, click Select to open the Select Database dialog box. Select the source database, and then return to the Choose Data Source dialog box.
5. Select the data source, and click OK to open the Choose Columns dialog box of the Query Wizard. Add the tables and fields you want to include in your result set. Click Next to open the Filter Data dialog box of the Query Wizard.
6. Specify the conditions you want the data to meet. Click Next to open the Sort Order dialog box of the Query Wizard.
7. Specify the sort order for the data. Click Next to open the Finish dialog box of the Query Wizard.
8. Select Return Data to Microsoft Office Excel. Click Finish to open the Import Data dialog box.
9. Specify whether you want to place the data in the existing worksheet or in a new worksheet.
10. Click OK to import the data.

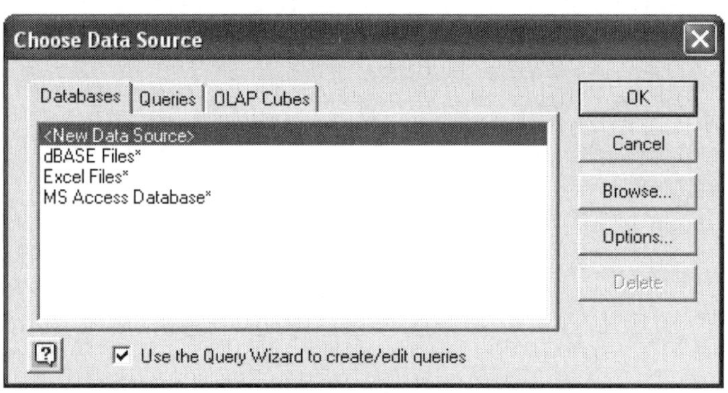

Exhibit 5-7: The Choose Data Source dialog box

Do it!

C-1: Using Microsoft Query to get data from an external database

Here's how	Here's why
1 Open Querying databases	(You might need to select Excel Files from the Files of type list in the Open dialog box.) This workbook contains two worksheets. QueryDb is the active sheet. You'll use the Microsoft Query program to retrieve data from an Access database and place it in this worksheet.
2 Save the workbook as **My querying databases**	In the current unit folder.
3 Activate the Data tab	
4 In the Get External Data group, click **From Other Sources**	To display a menu.
Choose **From Microsoft Query**	To open the Choose Data Source dialog box. By default, the Databases tab is active. You can either select an existing data source or create a new one.
5 Verify that <New Data Source> is selected	
Click **OK**	To open the Create New Data Source dialog box.
6 In the first box, enter **Employee**	To specify the name of the new data source.
In the second box, click the drop-down arrow and select the indicated option	(Scroll down.) To specify the database driver.

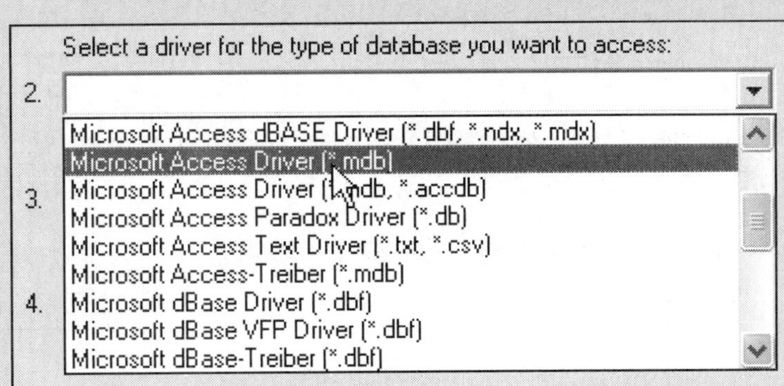

7	Click **Connect**	To open the ODBC Microsoft Access Setup dialog box.
	Under Database, click **Select**	To open the Select Database dialog box.
	From the Directories list, select the current unit folder	(If necessary.) To specify the folder that contains the database.
	From the Database Name list, select **Employee.mdb**	To specify the database from which you'll import data.
8	Click **OK**	To return to the ODBC Microsoft Access Setup dialog box.
	Click **OK**	To return to the Create New Data Source dialog box.
9	From the last list, select **Employees**	To specify which of the tables in the Employee database should act as the default for building queries.
	Click **OK**	To return to the Choose Data Source dialog box. The Employee data source has been added to the list and is selected.
10	Click **OK**	To close the Choose Data Source dialog box and open the Choose Columns dialog box of the Query Wizard. In the "Available tables and columns" list, Employees is selected.
	Click 	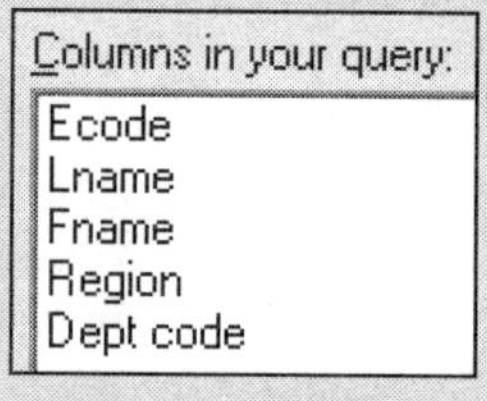 To include all columns of the Employees table in the query. The columns of the Employees table now appear in the "Columns in your query" list.

11 Click **Next**

To open the Filter Data dialog box of the Query Wizard. The group box under "Only include rows where" is not available and has no name.

From the Column to filter list, select **Dept code**

The group box under "Only include rows where" is now available and is named "Dept code." The first list under Dept code is also available.

From the first list under Dept code, select **equals**

To specify the comparison operator for the query.

From the second list under Dept code, select **MKTG**

This specifies that the result of this query will include only those rows where the Dept code is MKTG.

12 Click **Next**

To open the Sort Order dialog box of the Query Wizard.

From the Sort by list, select **Region**

This will sort data by Region. By default, Ascending is selected.

13 Click **Next**

To open the Finish dialog box of the Query Wizard. By default, Return Data to Microsoft Office Excel is selected.

14 Click **Finish**

The Import Data dialog box appears, prompting you to specify the destination for the data. Existing worksheet is selected by default.

15 Click **OK**

Ecode	Lname	Fname	Region	Dept code
E-09	Greg	Rita	East	MKTG
E-12	Austin	Rebecca	North	MKTG
E-10	Johnson	Trevor	South	MKTG
E-11	Anderson	Paul	West	MKTG

The records of all employees in the Marketing department appear in the worksheet.

16 Update the workbook

The Web query feature

Explanation

If you want to analyze data on the Web, such as online currency rates or stock quotes, you can create a Web query. When you run a Web query, Excel retrieves data that has been formatted with Hypertext Markup Language (HTML) or Extensible Markup Language (XML).

HTML and XML

The focus of HTML, which consists primarily of predefined tags, is the appearance of the content in a browser window. XML, on the other hand, focuses on the content and not on its appearance. There are no predefined tags in XML; instead, you create your own tags to give your data meaning and structure. Both markup languages are related to a parent language, SGML (Standard Generalized Markup Language), which provides rules for marking up documents and data.

Do it!

C-2: Discussing the Web query feature

Questions and answers

1 Which Excel feature do you use to analyze stock market quotes on the Web?

2 What are the file formats in which a Web query retrieves data?

3 What are the main differences between HTML and XML?

Use the Web query feature to retrieve data from the Web

Explanation

To retrieve data from a Web page:

1. Activate the Data tab. Then, in the Get External Data group, click From Web to open the New Web Query dialog box.
2. In the Address box, specify the address of the Web page from which you want to retrieve data, as shown in Exhibit 5-8.
3. Click the arrow next to the tables you want to select.
4. Click Options to open the Web Query Options dialog box. Select the format in which you want the data to be displayed. Click OK.
5. Click Import. In the Import Data dialog box, specify whether you want the data in an existing worksheet or a new worksheet. Click OK.

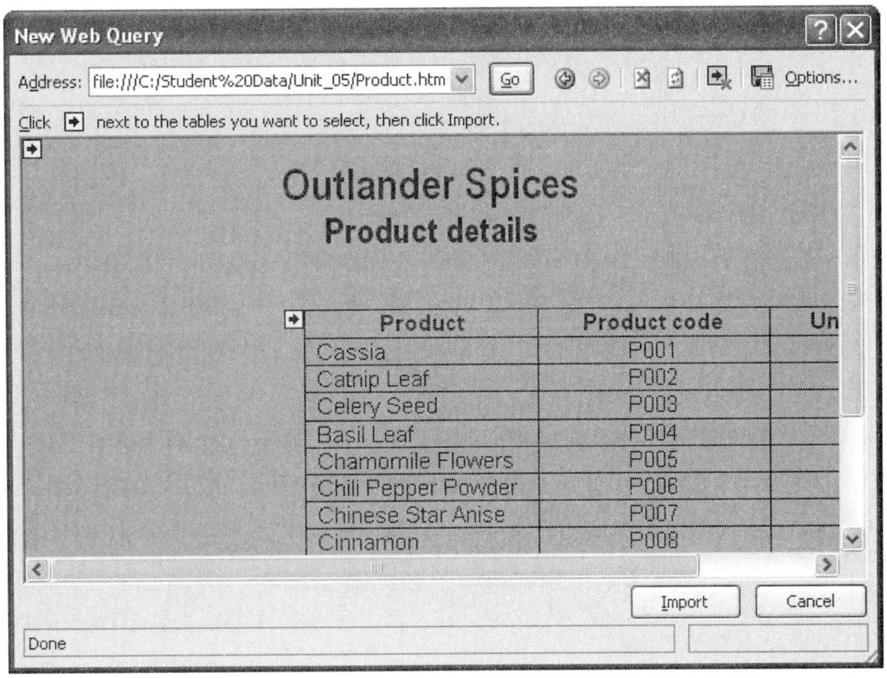

Exhibit 5-8: The New Web Query dialog box

Do it!

C-3: Using a Web query to get data from the Web

Here's how	Here's why
1 Activate the WebQ sheet	You'll use the Web query program to retrieve data from a Web page.
Activate the Data tab	If necessary.
2 In the Get External Data group, click **From Web**	To open the New Web Query dialog box.
3 In the Address box, enter **C:\Student Data\Unit_<##>\Product.htm**	(Substitute <##> with the current unit number.) This is the address of the Web page that contains the relevant data.
Click **Go**	The preview of the Web page appears in the dialog box.
4 Click the arrow to the left of the table, as shown	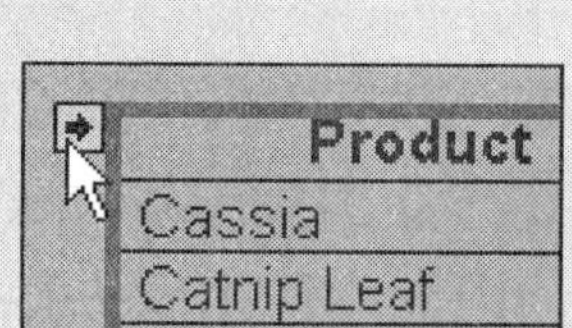 To import data from only the table on the Web page.
5 Click **Options** as shown	 To open the Web Query Options dialog box.
Under Formatting, select **Full HTML formatting**	To retain the current formatting of the table.
Click **OK**	
6 Click **Import**	To open the Import Data dialog box. By default, the Existing worksheet option is selected.
Click **OK**	The data from the table on the Web page appears in the worksheet.
7 Update and close the workbook	

Unit summary: Exporting and importing

Topic A In this topic, you learned how to **export data** from Excel to a text file. You learned how to **import data** from a text file into an Excel workbook. You also learned that you can separate the imported data into columns.

Topic B In this topic, you learned how to use the **XML Source task pane** to create an **XML map** for a workbook. You also learned how to use the XML Source task pane to import XML data into an Excel workbook and to export data from a workbook to an XML file. In addition, you learned how to delete XML maps.

Topic C In this topic, you learned how to use **Microsoft Query** to retrieve data from an Access database. You also learned how to use the **Web query** feature to retrieve data from Web pages in HTML or XML format.

Independent practice activity

In this activity, you'll export data from a worksheet to a text file. You'll create an XML map for a workbook. You'll also import an XML file and export data to an XML file. Finally, you'll work with data using Microsoft Query.

1. Open Exporting practice. (Ensure that Export is the active worksheet.)
2. Export data from the Export worksheet to a text file. Save the text file as **My exported text practice**. (*Hint:* When prompted, export only the current sheet.)
3. Open the exported file in Notepad. Because some product names are longer or shorter than others, the tabbed columns might not appear neat. Close Notepad.
4. Activate the XML worksheet. Create a workbook map by using EmployeeRecord, and link the elements in the file to the corresponding fields in the workbook. (*Hint:* In the XML Source task pane, click XML Maps.)
5. Import the EmployeeInfoPrac XML file.
6. Export the data in the XML worksheet as an XML file. Save the XML file as **My XML practice**.
7. Activate the Exporting practice worksheet. By using Microsoft Query, select or create an Employee database connection. (*Hint:* On the Data tab, in the Get External Data group, click From Other Sources and choose From Microsoft Query. If Employee does not appear in the Databases panel, select <New Data Source>; then click OK and enter data source information for the Employees database.)
8. Add all of the tables and columns (from Employees) to the query.
9. Include only those records with a Dept code value that equals SL.
10. Sort the data by the last name (Lname field), in ascending order.
11. Place the resulting data in cell A1 of the current sheet. (*Hint:* Check the result against Exhibit 5-9.)
12. Save the workbook as **My exporting practice**.
13. Close the XML Source task pane.
14. Close the workbook.

Ecode	Lname	Fname	Region	Dept code
E-02	Lee	Shannon	South	SL
E-03	McGregor	Melinda	West	SL
E-04	Overmire	James	North	SL
E-01	Pingault	Malcolm	East	SL

Exhibit 5-9: The worksheet as it appears after Step 12 of the independent practice activity

Review questions

1 An Excel workbook that's saved in a different file format will retain its original formatting. True or false?

2 List three ways that the XML Source task pane is useful.

3 How can you export a workbook to an XML file?

4 List the steps you would use to delete an XML map.

5 What is Microsoft Query?

Unit 6

Analytical options

Unit time: 50 minutes

Complete this unit, and you'll know how to:

A Use the Goal Seek and Solver utilities to meet a target output for a formula by adjusting the values in the input cells.

B Install and use the Analysis ToolPak.

C Create scenarios to save various sets of input values that produce different results.

D Create views to save different sets of worksheet display and print settings.

Topic A: Goal Seek and Solver

Explanation

You might want a formula to return a specific result, but you might not know the input values that will provide that result. For example, you might want to take out a loan for which the maximum monthly payment is $500. Based on this, you might want to know a possible combination of period, interest rate, and principal amount. In this case, you can use Goal Seek and Solver to find the input values.

What-if analysis

You can use the Goal Seek and Solver utilities to perform a *what-if analysis*. This type of analysis involves changing the values in a worksheet and observing how these changes affect the results of the formulas. You use Goal Seek to solve problems that have one variable. Use Solver to analyze problems that have multiple variables and constraints.

The Goal Seek utility

Use the Goal Seek utility to solve a formula based on the value that you want the formula to return. To use the Goal Seek utility:

1. Activate the Data tab.
2. In the Data Tools group, click What-If Analysis and choose Goal Seek to open the Goal Seek dialog box, shown in Exhibit 6-1.
3. In the Set cell box, specify the cell that contains the formula you want to solve.
4. In the To value box, enter the result you want.
5. In the By changing cell box, specify the cell that contains the value you want to adjust.
6. Click OK.

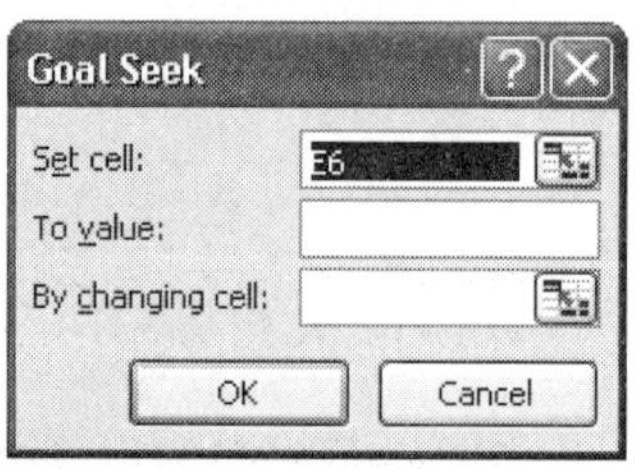

Exhibit 6-1: The Goal Seek dialog box

Do it!

A-1: Using Goal Seek to solve for a single variable

Here's how	Here's why
1 Open Analytical options	(From the current unit folder.) This workbook contains six worksheets. Goal seeking is the active sheet.
2 Save the workbook as **My analytical options**	In the current unit folder.
3 Select E6	This cell displays a monthly payment of -$3,417.76 for a loan amount of $100,000. You'll use Goal Seek to calculate the loan amount that you can obtain if you can afford a monthly payment of $10,000, given a period of 36 months and an interest rate of 14%.
Observe the formula bar	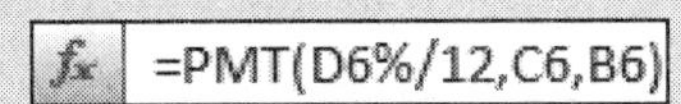 The PMT function calculates the monthly payment for the loan amount in B6 based on the annual interest rate in D6 and the repayment period in C6.
4 Activate the Data tab	
In the Data Tools group, click **What-If Analysis**	To display a menu.
Choose **Goal Seek...**	To open the Goal Seek dialog box, shown in Exhibit 6-1. The Set cell box displays E6. This cell contains the formula you want to solve.
5 In the To value box, enter **-10000**	This is the result you want the formula in E6 to return.
In the By changing cell box, enter **B6**	This is the cell containing the loan amount: the value that will be adjusted.
6 Click **OK**	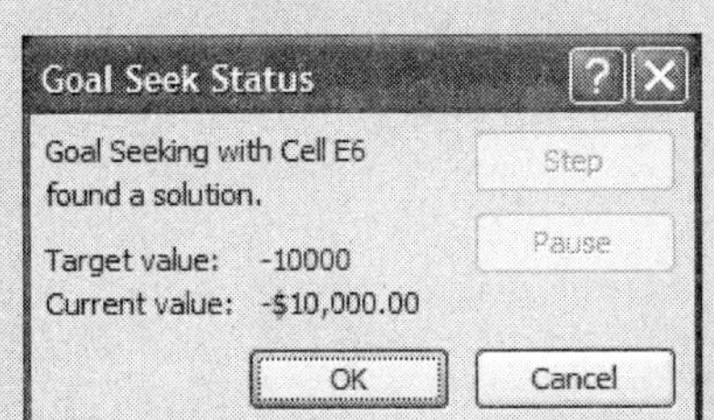 The Goal Seek Status dialog box opens. It tells you that Goal Seek has found a solution, which you can accept or reject. The target value represents the value you asked the formula to return. The current value represents the solution found by Goal Seek.

7 Click **OK**

To close the dialog box.

Loan amount (in $)	Period of repayment (in months)	Annual Rate of Interest (in %)	Monthly payment
$292,589	36	14	-$10,000.00

With a monthly payment of $10,000, a period of 36 months, and an interest rate of 14%, you can afford a loan of $292,589.

8 Find the loan amount that you can obtain from the NewCiti bank if you pay $15,000 per month for 42 months

(Use Goal Seek.) You'll get $487,820 as the loan amount.

9 Update the workbook

The Solver utility

Explanation

You use the Solver utility to perform complex what-if analyses. Solver helps you determine optimal values for a cell by adjusting multiple cells used in a formula. You can also apply multiple constraints to one or more cells used in a formula.

Although the Solver is a component of Excel, it is an add-in that isn't automatically installed. Therefore, to use it, you must first install it. To install the Solver and other add-ins:

1. Open the Excel Options dialog box.
2. From the category list, select Add-Ins.
3. From the Manage list, select Excel Add-ins and click Go to open the Add-Ins dialog box, shown in Exhibit 6-2.
4. Check the add-ins you want to install, and then click OK.
5. If necessary, close and restart Excel to display the Analysis group on the Data tab.

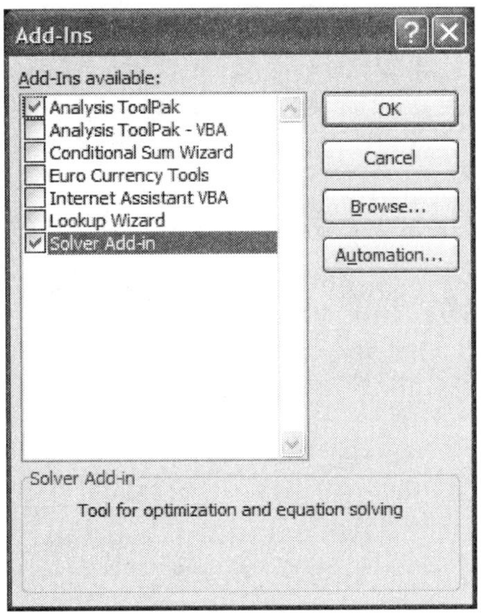

Exhibit 6-2: The Add-Ins dialog box

Do it!

A-2: Installing Solver and the Analysis ToolPak

Here's how	Here's why
1 Open the Excel Options dialog box	
Select **Add-Ins**	(In the category list on the left.) You'll add the Solver and Analysis ToolPak application extensions.
2 From the Manage list, select **Excel Add-ins**	If necessary.
Click **Go**	To open the Add-Ins dialog box.
Check **Analysis ToolPak** and **Solver Add-in**	
Click **OK**	To close the Add-Ins dialog box and to install the Analysis ToolPak. If a message box asks if you'd like to install this add-in now, click Yes. You might need to insert the Microsoft Office 2007 installation disk.
3 Close and restart Excel	(If necessary.) To display the Analysis group on the Data tab.

Using Solver

Explanation

After you install the Solver add-in, it's available on the Ribbon.

To use the Solver utility:

1 On the Data tab, in the Analysis group, click Solver to open the Solver Parameters dialog box, shown in Exhibit 6-3.
2 In the Set Target Cell box, specify the cell that contains the formula you want to solve.
3 Under Equal To, select the appropriate option—Max, Min, or Value of—for the result of the target cell.
4 In the By Changing Cells box, specify the cells in which the values will be adjusted.
5 In the Subject to the Constraints box, add any desired constraints by using the Add button. For example, if you were changing a cell that contained a period of months, you would want to constrain that cell to contain whole numbers.
6 Click Solve.

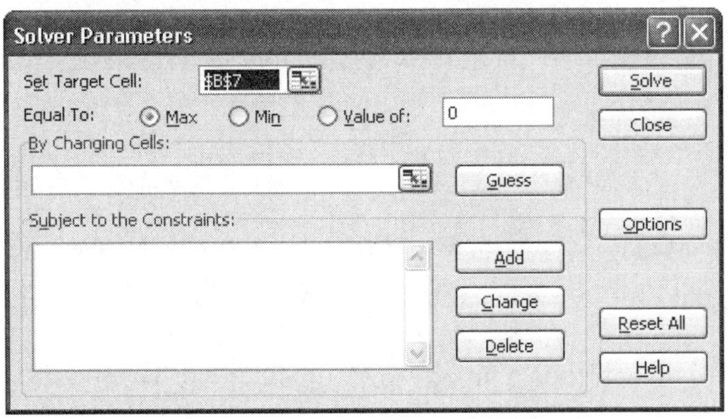

Exhibit 6-3: The Solver Parameters dialog box

Do it!

A-3: Using Solver to solve for multiple variables

Here's how	Here's why
1 Open My analytical options	Select the first item in the list of recent files.
Activate the Solver sheet	You'll use the Solver utility to minimize the company's advertising expenses while reaching an audience of one million people. You'll do this by adjusting the amounts spent on newspaper, radio, and TV ads.
2 Select each of the named ranges and observe the selected cells	This worksheet has ranges named Audience_reached, Max_impressions, Num_impressions, Spending, Total_audience, and Total_spending. The Solver will show these names, rather than cell notations, to make the information easier to understand.
3 Activate the Data tab	
In the Analysis group, click **Solver**	To open the Solver Parameters dialog box.
4 Select E15	(In the Solver sheet.) To enter it in the Set Target Cell box in the dialog box.
In the Equal To area, select **Min**	To specify that you want to minimize the total spending. The value in the Set Target Cell box changes to the cell's name, Total_spending.
5 Place the insertion point in the By Changing Cells box	These are the cell values the Solver will adjust.
Select **B14:D14**	(In the Solver sheet.) To make the Solver change these values to find the optimal advertising spending for each medium.
Press TAB	The value changes to the range's name, Num_impressions.
6 Under Subject to the Constraints, click **Add**	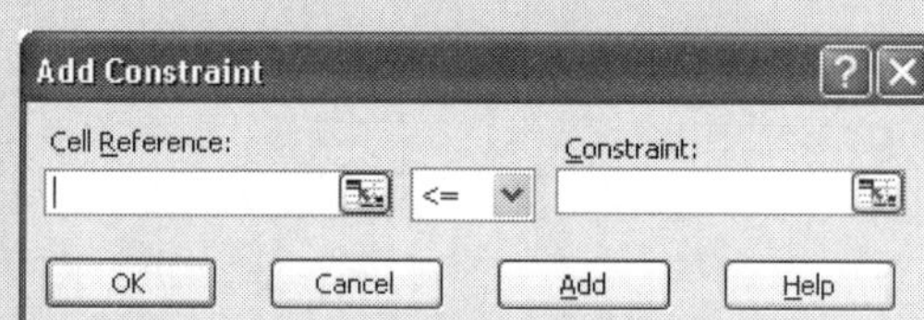 To open the Add Constraint dialog box. You'll specify limitations for cell values based on your objectives.

7	Select **E16**	The total audience reached must be greater than or equal to 2 million.
	From the comparison operator list, select **>=**	This is the greater-than-or-equal-to operator.
	In the Constraint box, enter **2000000**	
	Click **Add**	To add the constraint to the "Subject to the Constraints" list. The boxes in the Add Constraint dialog box are refreshed, and the insertion point is in the Cell Reference box.
8	Select **B14:D14**	The number of impressions for each cell in this range should be less than or equal to the maximum number of effective impressions listed above.
	In the list, verify that <= is selected	This is the less-than-or-equal-to operator.
	Select the Constraint box	
	Select **B10:D10**	This range and the selected operator specify that the number of impressions must be less than the maximum effective number.
9	Click **Add**	
10	Select **B14:D14**	The number of impressions must be an integer; you can't purchase a fraction of an ad impression.
	From the operator list, select **Int**	This is the integer operator.
	Click **OK**	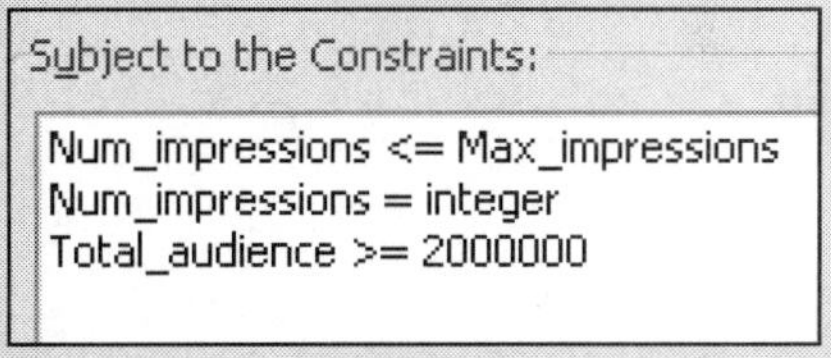 To add this third constraint to the "Subject to the Constraints" list and return to the Solver Parameters dialog box.

11 Click **Solve**	To make the Solver find a set of values for the number of impressions to minimize the cost. The Solver Results dialog box appears.
Observe the value in B14	The number of impressions for Newspaper is negative, which can't occur in real life. You'll change an option to prevent this problem.
Select **Restore Original Values**	In the Solver Results dialog box.
Click **OK**	
12 In the Analysis group, click **Solver**	To open the Solver Parameters dialog box. The parameters you selected appear.
Click **Options**	To open the Solver Options dialog box. You'll ensure that the Solver uses only positive spending values.
Check **Assume Non-Negative**	A negative value would represent income instead of spending.
Click **OK**	To close the Solver Options dialog box and return to the Solver Parameters dialog box.
13 Click **Solve**	To trigger Solver to adjust the values. After a moment, the Solver Results dialog box appears. Verify that Keep Solver Solution is selected. This ensures that the solution found by the Solver is retained.
Click **OK**	The adjusted values appear in the worksheet. E14 shows the total spending as $17,700. The value in E16 is 2,000,000, and the number-of-impressions values are integers that are less than the corresponding maximum-effective-impressions values.
14 Update the workbook	

Topic B: The Analysis ToolPak

Explanation

The Analysis ToolPak is a set of analysis tools, including Correlation, Covariance, Regression, and Sampling. Each tool consists of macro functions needed to perform the corresponding analysis. The following table lists the tools available in the ToolPak:

Analysis tool	Description
Anova	Performs variance analysis.
Correlation	Examines the relationship between two sets of data. Each set of data can have different units of measurement.
Covariance	Examines the relationship between two data ranges.
Descriptive Statistics	Summarizes information related to different types of data used in an analysis.
Exponential Smoothing	Adjusts the output based on previous forecasts.
F-Test Two Sample for Variances	Compares two population variances.
Fourier Analysis	Solves linear equations and analyzes periodic data by using the Fast Fourier Transform method.
Histogram	Determines the frequency of a value in a data range.
Moving Average	Forecasts values for a period based on the average of previous forecasts.
Random Number Generation	Generates random numbers based on several distributions to fill a range.
Rank and Percentile	Calculates the rank and percentile of each value in a data set.
Regression	Performs linear regression analysis to determine the relation between different values.
Sampling	Creates samples from a population.
t-Test	Tests the means of various populations.
z-Test	Tests the means of known variances.

Use analysis tools

After installing the Analysis ToolPak, you can select any tool from the Analysis Tools list. For example, you might want to create a sampling distribution for sales in a specific region for a specific year. To perform this analysis, you have to select samples from the sales report. You can use the Sampling analysis tool to get these samples from a data range. You can select data samples randomly or at regular intervals.

To select sample data by using the Sampling analysis tool:

1. Activate the Data tab.
2. In the Analysis group, click Data Analysis to open the Data Analysis dialog box.
3. From the Analysis Tools list, select Sampling, and then click OK to open the Sampling dialog box.
4. In the Input Range box, enter the range of data from which you want to select samples.
5. Specify a sampling method and an output option.
6. Click OK.

Do it!

B-1: Using the Sampling analysis tool

Here's how	Here's why
1 Activate the Sampling worksheet	Outlander Spices needs to audit 15 quarterly sales values for several stores. You won't analyze that data in this activity, but you will randomly select the 15 store and quarter combinations by using the Sampling analysis tool. The Sampling sheet contains a list of stores and quarters, with a combination of both combined in a column (because the Sampling tool requires that the information be numeric). For example, 203 represents store 002's third-quarter sales.
2 Activate the Data tab	If necessary.
In the Analysis group, click **Data Analysis**	To open the Data Analysis dialog box.
3 In the Analysis Tools list, select **Sampling**	You'll select data samples that represent sales in the East region.
Click **OK**	To open the Sampling dialog box.
4 In the Input Range box, enter **C7:C66**	(You can also click the Collapse Dialog button, select the range in the worksheet, and click the Expand Dialog button.) To specify the range of data from which samples are to be selected.
5 Under Sampling Method, select **Random**	(If necessary.) You'll select samples at random. Because the Sampling tool might repeat some values, you'll generate more than the target number of 15.
In the Number of Samples box, enter **20**	With 20 samples, 15 or more are likely to be unique.
6 Under Output options, select **Output Range**	You'll specify the range where the samples should appear. You can also display the output in a new worksheet or a new workbook.
In the Output Range box, enter **E7**	The output will begin in E7 and extend downward 20 rows.
7 Click **OK**	Data samples appear in E7:E22. Outlander Spices can now audit those quarterly sales values from the random sample you created.
8 Update the workbook	

Topic C: Scenarios

Explanation

Scenarios are sets of input values that produce different results. For example, in a budget projection worksheet, you can have one scenario that includes conservative sales figures and another scenario that includes more aggressive sales figures. Instead of creating new scenarios every time, you can modify existing scenarios. In a worksheet containing multiple scenarios, you can switch among them to view the results for different input values. In addition, you can merge scenarios from other worksheets.

Create a scenario

You can use the Scenario Manager dialog box to create a scenario. Here's how:

1. Activate the Data tab.
2. From the What-If Analysis menu in the Data Tools group, choose Scenario Manager to open the Scenario Manager dialog box.
3. Click the Add button to open the Add Scenario dialog box.
4. In the Scenario name box, enter a name for the scenario.
5. In the Changing cells box, specify the cells that contain the values you want to change. Click OK.
6. In the Scenario Values dialog box, specify values for the changing cells, and then click OK.

After creating the scenario, you can modify it by editing values for the changing cells. To edit values:

1. Open the Scenario Manager dialog box and select the scenario you want to change.
2. Click Edit to open the Edit Scenario dialog box.
3. Click OK to open the Scenario Values dialog box.
4. Specify values for the changing cells, and then click OK.

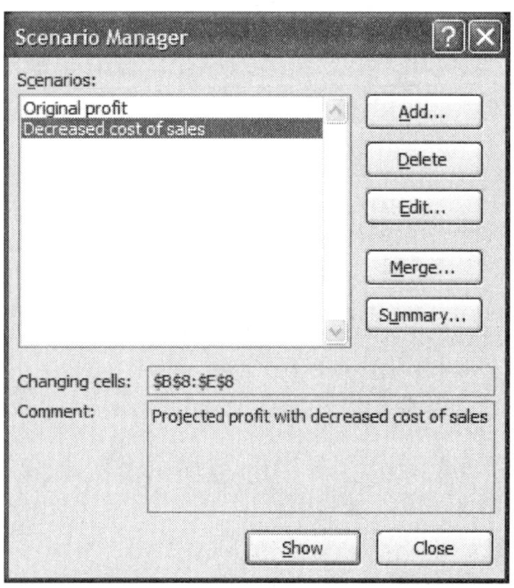

Exhibit 6-4: The Scenario Manager dialog box

Do it!

C-1: Creating scenarios

Here's how	Here's why
1 Activate the Scenarios sheet	You'll create scenarios for this worksheet to see how different Cost-of-sales values will affect the Gross profit, Net profit, and Profit %.
2 Select B8:E8	
Activate the Data tab	If necessary.
From the What-If Analysis menu in the Data Tools group, choose **Scenario Manager**	To open the Scenario Manager dialog box. A message is displayed, stating that no scenarios have been defined.
Click **Add**	To open the Add Scenario dialog box.
3 In the Scenario name box, enter **Original profit**	This is the name of the scenario that will preserve the original values. The Changing cells box displays the references of the selected cells.
Edit the Comment box to read **Original projected profit**	To describe the scenario.
Click **OK**	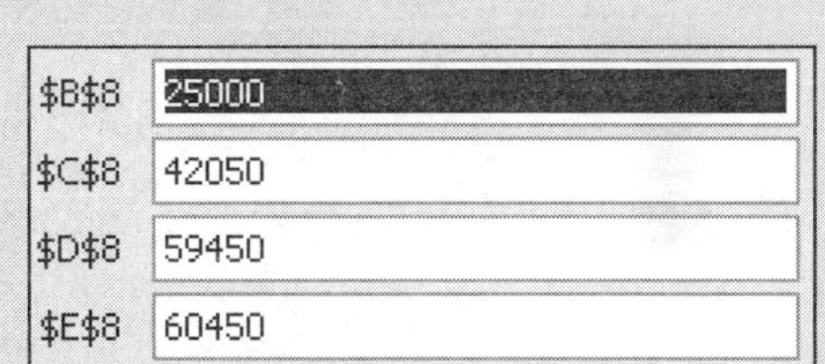 To open the Scenario Values dialog box. All of the boxes display the current values of the selected cells.
4 Click **Add**	To add the scenario Original profit to the Scenarios list and return to the Add Scenario dialog box. This scenario will preserve the original values in changing cells.
5 In the Scenario name box, enter **Decreased cost of sales**	This is the name of the scenario you are about to create.
Edit the Comment box to read **Projected profit with decreased cost of sales**	To describe the new scenario.
Click **OK**	To open the Scenario Values dialog box.
6 Enter the values as shown	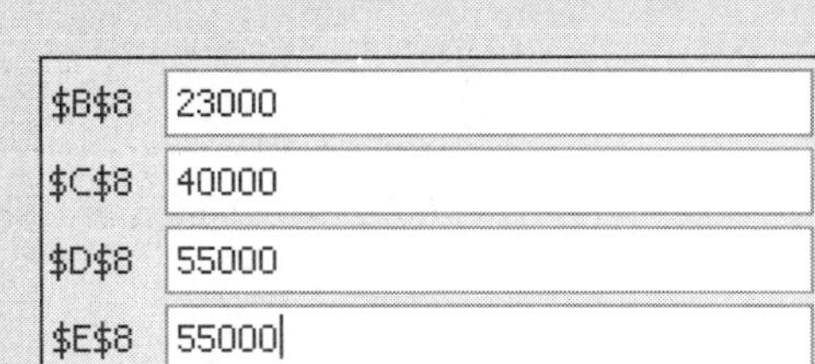

7	Click **OK**	To return to the Scenario Manager dialog box, as shown in Exhibit 6-4. The Scenarios list displays the names of the two scenarios you just defined.
8	Click **Show**	To apply the “Decreased cost of sales” scenario. The values in the range B8:E8 change according to the values stored in this scenario. Based on the new Cost-of-sales values, the values for Gross profit, Net profit, and Profit % also change. You’ll edit the scenario to lower the Cost-of-sales values even more.
	Click **Edit**	To open the Edit Scenario dialog box. The Scenario name box displays “Decreased cost of sales.”
	Click **OK**	To open the Scenario Values dialog box. All of the boxes display the current values of the selected cells.
9	Type the values shown	\$B\$8 20000 \$C\$8 35000 \$D\$8 50000 \$E\$8 48000
	Click **OK**	To return to the Scenario Manager dialog box.
	Click **Close**	
10	Update the workbook	

Switch among scenarios

Explanation

You can switch among scenarios to view results based on different input values. To display a scenario, open the Scenario Manager dialog box, select the name of the scenario you want to display, and click the Show button.

If you have a worksheet with many scenarios, you can switch among them more easily by adding the Scenario list to the Quick Access toolbar.

To add buttons to the Quick Access toolbar:

1. On the Quick Access toolbar, click Customize Quick Access Toolbar and choose More Commands. The Excel Options dialog box opens with the Customize pane displayed.
2. From the Available commands list, select the category that contains the command you want to add, or select All Commands. Some commands are available only in the list of all commands.
3. Select the command you want to add to the toolbar and click Add.
4. If desired, click Move Up or Move Down to change the command's position relative to the other commands on the toolbar.
5. Click OK to close the Excel Options dialog box.

Do it!

C-2: Switching among scenarios

Here's how	Here's why
1 Open the Scenario Manager dialog box	(Choose Scenario Manager from the What-If Analysis menu.) In the Scenarios list, "Decreased cost of sales" is selected by default.
Click **Show**	To apply the changes made in the scenario.
2 Click **Close**	The values for Cost of sales, Gross profit, Net profit, and Profit % have changed.
Observe F15	The Profit % has increased to 36.
	You'll add a Scenario Manager command to the Quick Access toolbar to make it more convenient to open that dialog box.
3 On the Quick Access toolbar, click as shown	
	To display the Customize Quick Access Toolbar menu.
Choose **More Commands...**	To open the Excel Options dialog box, with the Customize pane active.
4 From the Choose commands from list, select **Data tab**	The Scenario Manager is on the Data tab.
5 In the list of commands, select **Scenario Manager**	
Verify that "For all documents (default)" is selected in the Customize Quick Access Toolbar list	To ensure that the button you'll add is available in all documents, not just the active one.
Click **Add**	To add the command to the Quick Access toolbar.
	You'll also add a list of individual scenarios so you can choose between them without opening the Scenario Manager dialog box.
6 From the Choose commands from list, select **All commands**	
7 In the list of commands, select **Scenario**	
Click **Add**	To add the command to the Quick Access toolbar.
8 Click **OK**	To close the Excel Options dialog box.

9	On the Quick Access toolbar, click as shown	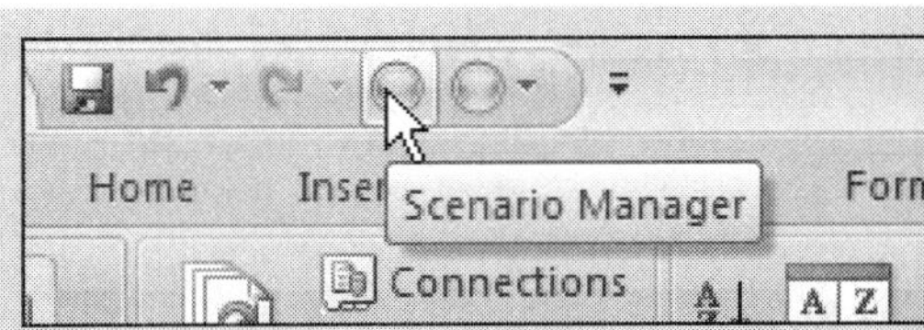 To open the Scenario Manager dialog box.
	Select **Original profit**	
	Click **Show**	To display the Original profit scenario.
	Click **Close**	
10	On the Quick Access toolbar, click as shown	 To display the Scenario list.
	Select **Decreased cost of sales**	You can use this list to switch among scenarios.
11	Update the workbook	

Merge scenarios

Explanation

You can merge scenarios from different worksheets so that all scenarios in a source worksheet are copied to the active worksheet. The changing cells in the active worksheet correspond to those in the source worksheet. This ensures that the changes made in the source worksheet are reflected in the active worksheet.

To merge scenarios:

1. Activate the worksheet where you want to merge scenarios.
2. Open the Scenario Manager dialog box.
3. Click Merge.
4. From the Sheet list, select the worksheet that contains the scenarios you want to merge.
5. Click OK.

The Scenario Summary report

A Scenario Summary report displays the original and current values for the changing cells corresponding to available scenarios. To create a Scenario Summary report:

1. Open the Scenario Manager dialog box.
2. Click Summary to open the Scenario Summary dialog box.
3. In the Result cells box, select the cells that contain the values changed by scenarios.
4. Click OK.

Do it!

C-3: Merging scenarios from another worksheet

Here's how	Here's why
1 Activate the Scenarios 2 sheet	You'll merge scenarios to this worksheet from the Scenarios worksheet.
2 Open the Scenario Manager dialog box	(Click the Scenario Manager button on the Quick Access toolbar.) There are no scenarios in the Scenarios 2 worksheet.
3 Click **Merge**	To open the Merge Scenarios dialog box. The Book box displays the name of the workbook from which you'll merge scenarios. The Sheet list contains the worksheets in the workbook. By default, Goal seeking is selected.
In the Sheet box, select **Scenarios**	You'll merge the scenarios in this worksheet.
4 Click **OK**	To return to the Scenario Manager dialog box. The Scenarios list displays the names of the two scenarios you just merged. By default, Original profit is selected.

5 Select **Decreased cost of sales**

Click **Show**	To apply the "Decreased cost of sales" scenario. The values for Cost of sales, Gross profit, Net profit, and Profit % change according to the values stored in the scenario.
Observe F15	The Profit % has increased to 36% in the Scenarios 2 worksheet.

6 Click **Summary**

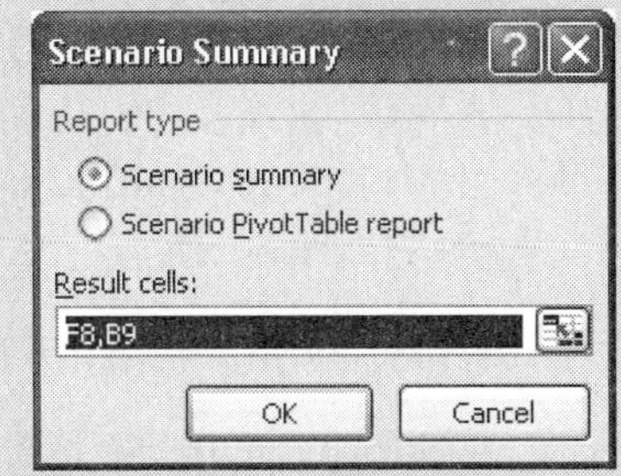

To open the Scenario Summary dialog box. By default, Scenario summary is selected.

In the worksheet, select E8	
Hold CTRL and select C9	To add it to the Result cells list. The values in these cells changed when you applied the "Decreased cost of sales" scenario.
Click **OK**	To create the Scenario Summary report in a new worksheet. You'll see the original and current values in the changing cells and result cells.

7 Update the workbook

Topic D: Views

Explanation

Views are sets of worksheet display and print settings that you can save. For example, in a sales worksheet, you can create a view in which the rows of data for all sales regions except for one are hidden. You can create multiple views for a worksheet and switch among them to change the display of the worksheet.

Create custom views

To create a view based on current display settings:

1. On the View tab, in the Workbook Views group, click Custom Views to open the Custom Views dialog box, shown in Exhibit 6-5.
2. Click Add to open the Add View dialog box.
3. In the Name box, type a name for the view. Click OK.

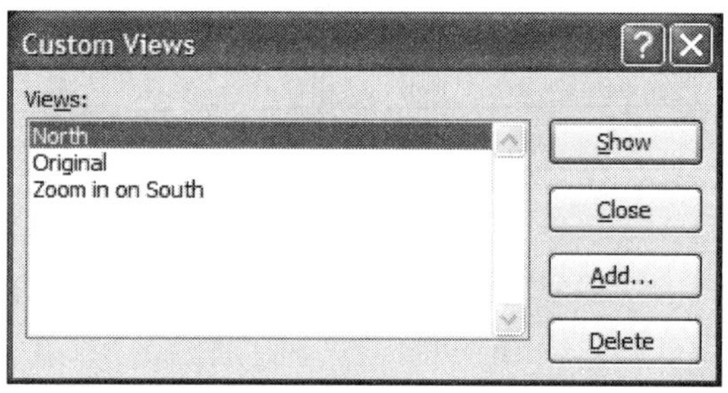

Exhibit 6-5: The Custom Views dialog box

Do it!

D-1: Creating views

Here's how	Here's why
1 Activate the View sheet	This worksheet contains a sales analysis report.
2 Activate the View tab	
3 In the Workbook Views group, click **Custom Views**	To open the Custom Views dialog box.
Click **Add**	To open the Add View dialog box.
4 In the Name box, enter **Original**	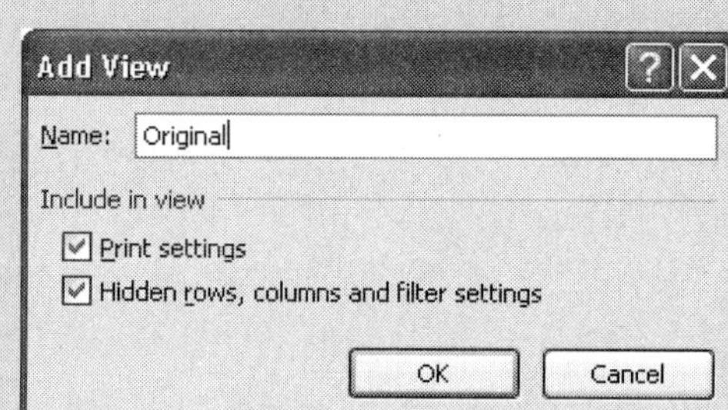
Click **OK**	

5	Select rows 1:3, 5:25, and 47:89	You'll need to press the Ctrl key and then select the rows.
	Activate the Home tab	
	In the Cells group, click **Format**	To display a menu.
	Choose **Hide & Unhide**, **Hide Rows**	To hide the selected rows. Now you can view only the records for the North region.
6	Open the Custom Views dialog box	Activate the View tab and click Custom Views.
	Click **Add**	To open the Add View dialog box.
7	In the Name box, enter **North**	
	Click **OK**	
8	Activate the Home tab	
	Click **Format**	In the Cells group.
	Choose **Hide & Unhide**, **Unhide Rows**	To display all the rows. The rows will not be displayed if you have selected anything in the worksheet after hiding the rows. In this case, press Ctrl+A to select all cells before choosing this command. A view also sets the scroll position and magnification. You'll create a view that zooms in on the South region without hiding the others.
9	Select A47	
	Scroll down so A47 is the top-left visible cell	
	In the status bar, click 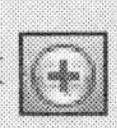 twice	To zoom in to 120%.
	Create a view named **Zoom in on South**	Use the Custom Views dialog box to add the view.
10	Update the workbook	

Switch among custom views

Explanation

To switch among views, open the Custom Views dialog box. From the Views list, select the view you want to display, and then click the Show button. You can also add the Custom Views command to the Quick Access toolbar to easily open that dialog box.

Do it!

D-2: Switching among views

Here's how	Here's why
1 Open the Custom Views dialog box	(In the Workbook Views group, click Custom Views") The Views list displays the names of all available views, as shown in Exhibit 6-5.
From the Views list, select **Original**	
Click **Show**	To display the records in Original view. Records for all of the regions appear in the worksheet.
2 Display the North view	Use the Custom Views dialog box.
Display the "Zoom in on South" view	
3 Update and close the workbook	

Unit summary: Analytical options

Topic A In this topic, you learned that you use **Goal Seek** to find a specific result for a formula by changing the value of one of the input cells. You also learned that you use the **Solver** add-in to determine optimal values for a cell by changing the values of multiple cells used in a formula.

Topic B In this topic, you learned how to install and use the **Analysis ToolPak**. You also learned how to use the **Sampling analysis tool** to select samples from a data range.

Topic C In this topic, you learned how to create and edit **scenarios**. You learned that scenarios are used to save sets of input values that produce different results. Then, you learned how to **switch among scenarios** to view different data results in a worksheet. In addition, you learned how to **merge scenarios** and create a **Scenario Summary report**.

Topic D In this topic, you learned how to create **views**. You learned that views are created to save different sets of worksheet display and print settings. You also learned how to switch among views and learned how doing this changes the display of a worksheet.

Independent practice activity

In this activity, you'll use Goal Seek and Solver to calculate values. You'll also create and display several views.

1 Open Analytical options practice. Goal seeking should be the active worksheet.

2 Save the workbook as **My analytical options practice**.

3 In D6, use Goal Seek to calculate the loan amount in C6 for a monthly deduction of $2,300. (*Hint:* Use the Goal Seek dialog box. The loan amount will be $108,250.)

4 Activate the Solver worksheet. Use Solver to calculate a total profit of 30% by adjusting the values for Total sales, Cost of sales, Overhead, and Marketing. When adjusting values, you must ensure that the total overhead for the year cannot be greater than $25,000, and the net profit for the year must be at least $100,000. Compare your results with Exhibit 6-6. (*Hint:* The Solver Parameters dialog box should look like the one shown in Exhibit 6-7.)

5 Update the workbook.

6 In the Views worksheet, create views named **Accounting**, **Customer support**, **Human resources**, **Marketing**, and **National sales**. Each view should display the details for the respective departments. Display each view.

7 Update and close the workbook.

	Qtr1	Qtr2	Qtr3	Qtr4	Total
Total sales	$56,202	$84,402	$95,702	$97,452	$333,758
Cost of sales	$38,213	$40,957	$58,357	$59,357	$196,884
Gross profit	$17,989	$43,445	$37,345	$38,095	$136,874
Overhead	$6,407	$6,427	$4,527	$2,427	$19,788
Marketing	$5,907	$5,537	$3,407	$2,107	$16,958
	$12,314	$11,964	$7,934	$4,534	$36,747
Net profit	$5,675	$31,481	$29,411	$33,561	$100,128
Profit %	10	37	31	34	30

Exhibit 6-6: The Solver worksheet after Step 4 of the independent practice activity

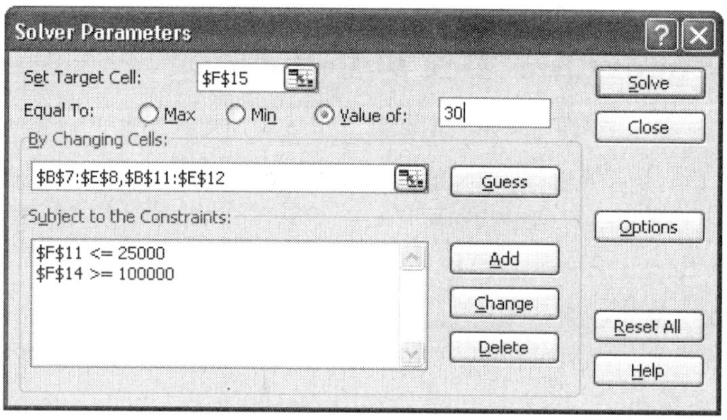

Exhibit 6-7: The Solver Parameters dialog box after Step 4 of the independent practice activity

Review questions

1 What utilities can be used to perform what-if analysis?

2 Which utility solves a formula based on the value that you want the formula to return?

3 List the steps you would use to install the Analysis ToolPak.

4 What are scenarios?

5 List the steps you would use to change a scenario.

Unit 7

Macros and custom functions

Unit time: 45 minutes

Complete this unit, and you'll know how to:

A Create and run macros to automate complex and repetitive tasks.

B Use the Visual Basic Editor to edit a macro.

C Create custom functions.

Topic A: Running and recording a macro

This topic covers the following Microsoft Certified Application Specialist exam objective for Excel 2007.

#	Objective
5.4.2	**Using the correct format, save a workbook as a template, a Web page, a macro-enabled document, or another appropriate document.** • Save as a macro-enabled workbook

Explanation

You can use macros to automate complex and repetitive tasks. A *macro* is a series of instructions that execute automatically with a single command. For example, you can create a macro to format a worksheet or to print a report. You can use the macros already available in Excel or create your own. To make macros more convenient to use, you can assign them to Quick Access toolbar buttons.

Run macros

To run a macro, activate the Developer tab. In the Code group, click Macros to open the Macro dialog box, shown in Exhibit 7-1. Select the desired macro and click Run.

Exhibit 7-1: The Macro dialog box

Enabling macros

Macros can contain viruses that can harm your computer. To prevent this problem, by default Excel requires you to enable macros after opening a file that contains them. To enable macros, click More Options in the Security Warning bar that appears, and then click Enable this content.

If Windows is set to display file-name extensions, you can use them to distinguish an Excel file that contains macros from an Excel file without macros. A standard Excel 2007 file uses the extension .xlsx; an Excel 2007 file with macro code uses the extension .xlsm.

Trust Center settings

You can protect your workbook by setting a macro security level. The security levels available are:

- **High** — Disables macros when you open a workbook.
- **Medium** — Prompts you to either enable or disable macros.
- **Low** — Enables macros automatically when you open a workbook.

To set the macro security level, click Trust Center on the Security Warning bar that appears when you open a file that contains macros, or click Macro Settings in the Code group on the Developer tab.

Do it!

A-1: Running a macro

Here's how	Here's why
1 Open Running macros	(From the current unit folder.) This document contains macros, which are disabled by default. You'll enable the macros so you can run them.
In the Security Warning bar that appears, click **Options**	(Above the formula bar.) To open the Security Alert - Macro dialog box.
Select **Enable this content**	To enable the macros included in the workbook.
Click **OK**	To close the Trust In Office dialog box and return to the workbook.
2 Open the Save As dialog box	
In the File name box, enter **My running macros**	
Observe that Excel Macro-Enabled Workbook appears in the Save as type list	Excel 2007 files with macros are saved as a different file type, with the extension .xlsm instead of .xlsx.
Click **Save**	To save the file in the current unit folder.
3 Select A4:D4	You'll run the Wrap_text macro to wrap the text in the selected cells.
On the Developer tab, in the Code group, click **Macros**	To open the Macro dialog box. It displays the names of available macros, as shown in Exhibit 7-1.
Observe that the Column_titles macro is selected	
Click **Run**	To run the macro. Notice that the text in the cells is wrapped to multiple lines as necessary, bottom-aligned, and bold.
4 Select E4	The macros in this workbook were assigned shortcut keys. You'll use one to run the Column_titles macro.
Press CTRL + SHIFT + C	The text is formatted to match the other column titles.

5 Select E5	
Run the Monthly_deduction macro	(Use the Macro dialog box.) The monthly deduction amount appears in E5.
Select E5	The formula for the PMT function appears in the formula bar. This formula was entered by the macro you just ran.
6 Display the monthly deduction for James Overmire in E6	Use the shortcut key Ctrl+Shift+M to run the Monthly_deduction macro.
7 Update and close the workbook	

Record macros

Explanation

To create a macro, you can either program it by typing Visual Basic code, or you can have Excel record actions as you perform them. Recording is simpler, but creates more lines of code; this can be less efficient if you want to edit the macro later.

To record a macro:

1. In the status bar, click the Record Macro button to open the Record Macro dialog box.
2. Specify a macro name and a shortcut key. Macro names can include letters, numbers, and underscores, must begin with a letter, and cannot contain spaces.
3. Click OK to start recording the macro.
4. Perform the actions you want to include in the macro. As you work, Excel records the sequence of steps.
5. When you're finished, click the Stop Recording button in the status bar.

Saving files with macros

When you add a macro to a file that didn't contain any previously and you then save the file, Excel displays a dialog box that warns you that it will save the file without macros. The default response, Yes, will delete any macros you've recorded. Click No to stop saving; then choose File, Save As and save the file in the Excel Workbook (code) format.

Do it!

A-2: Recording a macro

<table>
<tr><th>Here's how</th><th>Here's why</th></tr>
<tr><td>1 Open Macros</td><td>You'll record a macro to format column titles.</td></tr>
<tr><td>2 Save the workbook as
My macros</td><td></td></tr>
<tr><td>3 Select E4</td><td>This cell should be formatted as a column heading. When you want a macro to be associated with a particular cell, select that cell before turning on the recorder.</td></tr>
<tr><td>In the status bar, click as shown</td><td>

To open the Record Macro dialog box.</td></tr>
<tr><td>4 Edit the Macro name box to read
Column_titles</td><td></td></tr>
<tr><td>Click in the Shortcut key box</td><td></td></tr>
<tr><td>Press SHIFT + C</td><td>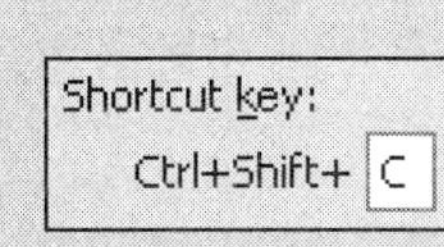

To define the shortcut key for the Column_titles macro as Ctrl+Shift+C. (Excel adds the Ctrl part.)</td></tr>
<tr><td>In the Store macro in list, verify that This Workbook is selected</td><td>To specify that the macro will be stored in only the active workbook.</td></tr>
<tr><td>In the Description box, enter
Wrap text, bottom align, and boldface selected cells.</td><td></td></tr>
<tr><td>5 Click **OK**</td><td>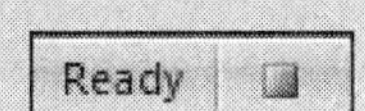

The Stop Recording button appears in the status bar.</td></tr>
</table>

6	Activate the Home tab	If necessary.
	In the Alignment group, click	(The Wrap Text button.) To make the text wrap to multiple lines.
	Click	To left-align the text in the cell.
	Click	To position the text at the bottom of the cell.
	In the Font group, click **B**	To apply bold formatting. You've completed all the steps you want the macro to perform.
7	In the status bar, click	To stop recording.
8	Save the workbook as **My recorded macros**	

		A dialog box appears, warning you that you can't save a file with a macro in a standard workbook file.
	Click **No**	The Save As dialog box opens.
9	From the Save as type list, select **Excel Macro-Enabled Workbook**	To save the file as a workbook with code.
	Click **Save**	To update the workbook and close the dialog box.
10	Select A4	(If necessary.) You'll test the macro you recorded.
	Run the Column_titles macro	(Press Ctrl+Shift+C.) The title is formatted as you specified.
11	Update the workbook	

Assign macros to buttons

Explanation

There are several ways to run a macro. One of them is to assign a macro to a button on the Quick Access toolbar. After assigning the macro to a button, you can run it by clicking that button.

To assign a macro to a button:

1. Click Customize Quick Access Toolbar and choose More Commands. The Excel Options dialog box opens with the Customize pane displayed.
2. From the Choose commands from list, select Macros.
3. Select the macro you want to add to the toolbar and click Add >>.
4. Click OK.

Do it!

A-3: Assigning a macro to a button

Here's how	Here's why
1 On the Quick Access toolbar, click as shown	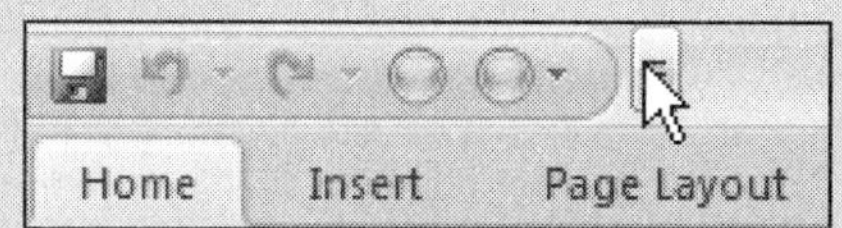 (Customize Quick Access Toolbar.) To display a menu.
Choose **More Commands...**	To open the Excel Options dialog box with the Customize screen displayed.
2 From the Choose commands from list, select **Macros**	To display a list of available macros. The macro you created appears in the list.
Select **Column_titles**	
Click **Add >>**	To add the macro button to the Quick Access toolbar.
3 Click **OK**	To close the dialog box. You'll test the button on another column title.
4 Select B4	
On the Quick Access toolbar, click 	To run the macro on the selected cell.
5 Update the workbook	

Topic B: Working with VBA code

Explanation

Excel saves the steps in a macro as Visual Basic for Applications (VBA) code. You can view and edit the code of a macro with the Visual Basic Editor.

VBA code is stored in special sheets called modules. A *module* might contain one or more sub procedures. A *sub procedure* is a named block of lines of code which, when executed, perform a sequence of steps.

Examine VBA code

VBA code consists of statements and comments. *Statements* are instructions that perform certain actions. *Comments* are non-executable lines of text used to describe sections of macro code. Comments begin with a single apostrophe.

The following table describes the components of a statement:

Item	Description
Keywords	Special VBA terms that, by default, appear in blue. For example, the `Sub` keyword marks the beginning of a sub procedure, and the `End Sub` keyword marks the end of a sub procedure.
Variables	Used to store values. For example, you can use variables to store the results of a formula.
Operators	Used just as they are in a worksheet. Operators can be arithmetic (+, -, /, *) or comparison (=, >, <).
Procedure call	A statement that calls a procedure from another procedure. You can do this by inserting the name of the first procedure into the second procedure.

Observe a VBA code module

To observe a VBA code module, open the Macro dialog box. Then, click the Edit button to open the Microsoft Visual Basic window.

Do it!

B-1: Observing a VBA code module

Here's how	Here's why
1 Open the Macro dialog box	(On the Developer tab, in the Code group, click Macros.) By default, Column_titles is selected in the Macro name list.
Click **Edit**	To open the Microsoft Visual Basic window. The name of the workbook appears in the title bar.
Observe the Code window	This window displays the code for the Column_titles macro.
2 Observe the first line in the Code window	`Sub Column_titles()` The `Sub` keyword marks the beginning of the macro. Keywords are blue.
Observe the last line in the Code window	`End Sub` The `End Sub` keyword marks the end of the macro.

3 Observe the comments	`' Column_titles Macro`
	`' Wrap text, bottom align, and boldface`
	`'`
	`' Keyboard Shortcut: Ctrl+Shift+C`
	Comments begin with an apostrophe and describe the macro. By default, comments are green.

4 Observe the statements	Statements appear in black and instruct Excel to perform a sequence of actions. The statements are located between the `Sub` and `End Sub` keywords.
Observe the indented statement lines between the first set of `With Selection` and `End With` lines	Each group of lines between the `With Selection` and `End With` statements applies to the selected cells. Sophisticated macros can select cells other than the ones originally selected when the macro was created.
Observe the repeats of the `With Selection/End With` blocks	Each time you clicked a button in the Alignment group, the macro recorded all of the alignment settings. This isn't an efficient use of code because many of the lines are repeated.

Edit VBA code

Explanation

Sometimes you might need to edit the code of a macro. For example, say you have a macro that calculates the monthly deduction at an interest rate of 12%, and you want to change the interest rate to 11%. Instead of recording a new macro, you can edit the VBA code of the existing macro.

You can edit macro code in the Visual Basic Editor. Make sure to save the macro after you've made any necessary changes.

Do it!

B-2: Editing VBA code

Here's how	Here's why
1 Compare the `.WrapText`, `.HorizontalAlignment`, and `.VerticalAlignment` lines in the three `With Selection` blocks of code	Excel created each block of code when you clicked a button in the Alignment group. The first block set the `.WrapText` value to `True`, the second block set the `.HorizontalAlignment` value to `xlLeft`, and the third block set the `.VerticalAlignment` setting to `xlBottom`. Because the third block contains the settings you chose for the first two, the first two are redundant. You'll delete them to make the code more efficient.
2 Select from the first instance of `With Selection` through the second instance of `End With`, as shown	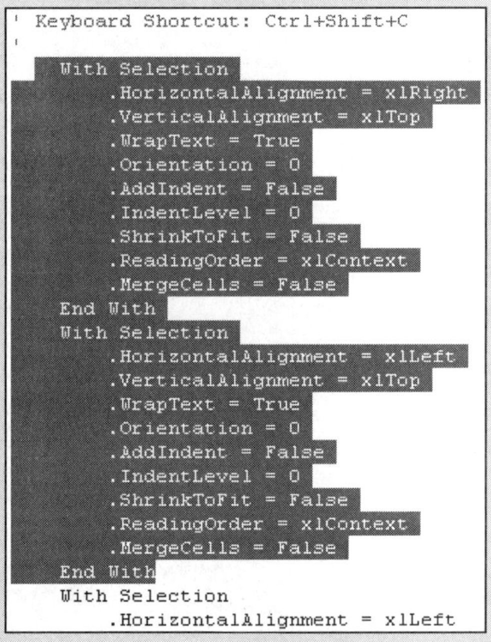 ' Keyboard Shortcut: Ctrl+Shift+C ' With Selection .HorizontalAlignment = xlRight .VerticalAlignment = xlTop .WrapText = True .Orientation = 0 .AddIndent = False .IndentLevel = 0 .ShrinkToFit = False .ReadingOrder = xlContext .MergeCells = False End With With Selection .HorizontalAlignment = xlLeft .VerticalAlignment = xlTop .WrapText = True .Orientation = 0 .AddIndent = False .IndentLevel = 0 .ShrinkToFit = False .ReadingOrder = xlContext .MergeCells = False End With With Selection .HorizontalAlignment = xlLeft These blocks of code are no longer necessary.
3 Press DELETE	To delete the selected code. You've decided that you don't want the macro to change the horizontal alignment, so you'll delete that code as well.

4 Delete the following line:

```
.HorizontalAlignment = xlLeft
```

Compare your code with the code shown

```
' Keyboard Shortcut: Ctrl+Shift+C
'

    With Selection
        .VerticalAlignment = xlBottom
        .WrapText = True
        .Orientation = 0
        .AddIndent = False
        .IndentLevel = 0
        .ShrinkToFit = False
        .ReadingOrder = xlContext
        .MergeCells = False
    End With
    Selection.Font.Bold = True
End Sub
```

5 Update the code and close the Microsoft Visual Basic window

6 Select C4:D4 and run the Column_titles macro

The text is formatted and retains its original horizontal alignment.

7 Update the workbook

Topic C: Creating functions

Explanation

A *function procedure* is similar to a sub procedure except that it returns a value on execution. All of the built-in functions of Excel, such as SUM and AVERAGE, are written by using function procedures.

You can also create functions to meet your specific needs. Such functions are called *custom functions*. For example, you can create a function that calculates commissions for salespeople based on their total sales.

Custom functions

You create custom functions in a Visual Basic module. In a custom function, you can include mathematical expressions, built-in Excel functions, and Visual Basic code. You can create custom functions to work with text, numbers, or dates.

You use custom functions in the same way you use built-in functions. You can also supply values to a custom function. That function then performs calculations on those values and returns a result.

Parts of a custom function

Examine the following code:

```
Function Profit(sales, cost)
Profit=sales-cost
End Function
```

Here, the `Function` keyword marks the beginning of the function. `Profit` is the name of the function, and the `End Function` keyword marks the end of the function.

Arguments are the values that a function uses for calculations. Arguments are specified in parentheses after the function name. In the preceding code, `sales` and `cost` are the arguments of the Profit function.

A *return value* is the value returned by a function after execution. You specify the return value by equating the function name to the value it must return. This is shown in the second statement of the preceding code.

Creating modules

A workbook can contain more than one Visual Basic module. Adding modules can help you organize code if you've created many macros or custom functions. To create an additional module, in the Microsoft Visual Basic window, choose Insert, Module.

Do it!

C-1: Creating a custom function

Here's how	Here's why
1 Activate the Developer tab	If necessary.
2 In the Code group, click **Visual Basic**	To open the Microsoft Visual Basic window.
3 Choose **Insert**, **Module** 	To add a module sheet. In the title bar, Module2 indicates that this is the second module in the My recorded macros workbook.
4 Place the insertion point in the Code window	If necessary.
5 Enter the following code: `Function MyDeduction(loan_amt, num_pmts)`	This code defines a function named `MyDeduction` in which `loan_amt` and `num_pmts` are the arguments.
Press ENTER	To move to the next row. The keyword `End Function` appears automatically at the end.
6 Enter the following code: `MyDeduction = -pmt(0.1/12, num_pmts, loan_amt)`	This code calculates the payment based on 10% annual interest (expressed as 0.1 divided by 12 months), and returns the result.
7 Update the code	
Close the Microsoft Visual Basic window	
8 In E5, enter **=MyDeduction(C5,D5)**	The payment of $1,816.62 appears in E5.
9 Update and close the workbook	

Unit summary: Macros and custom functions

Topic A

In this topic, you learned how to record and run a **macro**. You learned that macros perform tasks automatically and can be created to meet your specific needs. Then, you learned how to assign a macro to a button and run the macro by clicking that button.

Topic B

In this topic, you learned that macros are saved as **VBA code**, and you examined some VBA code. Then, you learned how to edit the code for a macro.

Topic C

In this topic, you learned how to create a **custom function**. You learned that custom functions are used to perform calculations when built-in functions are not available.

Independent practice activity

In this activity, you'll record, edit, and run several macros.

1 Open Macros practice. (The Macros worksheet contains two scenarios: Original and Lower cost of sales. To access these scenarios, you'll activate the Data tab.)

2 Save the workbook as **My macros practice** in the Excel Macro-Enabled Workbook file format.

3 Record a macro named **Display_lower_cost_of_sales** that has Ctrl+Shift+C as its shortcut key. This macro should show the "Lower cost of sales" scenario.

To do this, start recording the macro. Activate the Data tab, and in the Data Tools group, click What-If Analysis and choose Scenario Manager. In the Scenarios list, select **Lower cost of sales**, and then click **Show**. Click **Close**; then stop recording the macro.

4 Record a macro named **Display_original** that has Ctrl+Shift+O as its shortcut key. This macro should show the Original scenario.

5 Run the Display_lower_cost_of_sales macro. Run the Display_original macro.

6 Change the name of the "Lower cost of sales" scenario to **Decreased cost of sales**. (*Hint:* Open the Scenario Manager dialog box, select **Lower cost of sales** from the Scenarios list, and click **Edit**. Do not change any other values.)

7 Edit the VBA code for the Display_lower_cost_of_sales macro to show the Decreased cost of sales scenario. Close the Microsoft Visual Basic window. (*Hint:* Open the Macro dialog box, select the macro, and click **Edit**. In the Display_lower_cost_of_sales macro, edit the argument of the ActiveSheet.Scenarios function to read **Decreased cost of sales**.)

8 Run the edited macro.

9 Update the workbook and close it.

Review questions

1 What is a macro?

2 List two ways to create a macro.

3 In what type of code, or language, does Excel save macros? Where can you view and edit this code?

4 What is unique about a function procedure?

5 How do you specify a return value in a function?

Unit 8

Conditional formatting and SmartArt

Unit time: 50 minutes

Complete this unit, and you'll know how to:

A Apply three kinds of conditional formatting (data bars, icon sets, and color scales) to represent cell data in graphical form.

B Insert and modify SmartArt graphics.

Topic A: Conditional formatting with graphics

This topic covers the following Microsoft Certified Application Specialist exam objective for Excel 2007.

#	Objective
4.3.3	**Apply the following conditional formats:** • Data Bars • Color Scales • Icon Sets

Conditional formatting options

Explanation

In addition to simply applying basic Excel formats such as fills and font colors, conditional formatting can help you represent data in graphical form. You can create data bars and icon sets to depict values or divide them into categories. In addition, you can use data bars and icon sets to compare column values to one another. You can also use color scales to format cells differently depending on their values.

Data bars

You can create the effect of a bar chart superimposed on a table of values by applying *data bars*. As shown in Exhibit 8-1, data bars show the values in cells relative to other cells in a range. A data bar's length represents the cell's value.

		Sales per quarter				
Salesperson	Rating	Qtr1	Qtr2	Qtr3	Qtr4	Total sales
Bill MacArthur		$1,500	$1,750	$1,500	$2,700	$7,450
Jamie Morrison		$3,560	$3,000	$1,700	$2,000	$10,260
Maureen O'Connor		$4,500	$4,000	$3,500	$3,700	$15,700
Rebecca Austin		$3,250	$2,725	$3,000	$3,250	$12,225
Paul Anderson		$2,520	$2,000	$2,500	$2,700	$9,720
Cynthia Roberts		$1,500	$1,700	$1,800	$2,000	$7,000
Rita Greg		$4,590	$4,050	$4,500	$3,700	$16,840
Trevor Johnson		$3,660	$3,200	$3,000	$2,250	$12,110
Kevin Meyers		$1,790	$1,800	$2,000	$2,200	$7,790
Adam Long		$1,700	$1,950	$2,500	$2,750	$8,900
Kendra James		$1,650	$2,000	$1,500	$1,750	$6,900
Michael Lee		$2,050	$2,500	$2,800	$3,200	$10,550
Sandra Lawrence		$3,425	$3,750	$4,000	$3,120	$14,295
Mary Smith		$4,540	$2,700	$3,000	$3,200	$13,440
Annie Philips		$1,200	$1,700	$1,800	$2,000	$6,700

Exhibit 8-1: Data bars representing the values in a range

It's often helpful to widen the column in which you apply data bars. The bars' lengths are affected by the column width.

To create data bars:

1 Activate the Home tab.

2 Select the range of cells in which you want to display data bars.

3 In the Styles group, click Conditional Formatting to display a menu. Then choose Data Bars and select an option.

Editing conditional formatting rules

Although the choices in the Conditional Formatting menu might serve your needs much of the time, you might want to fine-tune a few things, such as which cells are affected and what they look like. For example, by default, the smallest value in a range will display a very short bar, while the largest value will display the longest bar. While this approach depicts the *spread* of values, it doesn't necessarily accurately represent the differences among them.

For example, if all of the values are between 900 and 1000, the differences in bar length will appear dramatically larger than they would with bars drawn on a scale of 0 to 1000. You can set parameters for the shortest and longest data bars based on numeric values, percentiles, percents, or even custom formulas. Exhibit 8-2 shows data bars based on a range from zero to the largest value. Compare these bars with those shown in Exhibit 8-1 to see the effect of the Shortest Bar setting. The setting you choose depends on what you want to communicate.

		Sales per quarter				
Salesperson	**Rating**	**Qtr1**	**Qtr2**	**Qtr3**	**Qtr4**	**Total sales**
Bill MacArthur		$1,500	$1,750	$1,500	$2,700	$7,450
Jamie Morrison		$3,560	$3,000	$1,700	$2,000	$10,260
Maureen O'Connor		$4,500	$4,000	$3,500	$3,700	$15,700
Rebecca Austin		$3,250	$2,725	$3,000	$3,250	$12,225
Paul Anderson		$2,520	$2,000	$2,500	$2,700	$9,720
Cynthia Roberts		$1,500	$1,700	$1,800	$2,000	$7,000
Rita Greg		$4,590	$4,050	$4,500	$3,700	$16,840
Trevor Johnson		$3,660	$3,200	$3,000	$2,250	$12,110
Kevin Meyers		$1,790	$1,800	$2,000	$2,200	$7,790
Adam Long		$1,700	$1,950	$2,500	$2,750	$8,900
Kendra James		$1,650	$2,000	$1,500	$1,750	$6,900
Michael Lee		$2,050	$2,500	$2,800	$3,200	$10,550
Sandra Lawrence		$3,425	$3,750	$4,000	$3,120	$14,295
Mary Smith		$4,540	$2,700	$3,000	$3,200	$13,440
Annie Philips		$1,200	$1,700	$1,800	$2,000	$6,700

Exhibit 8-2: Adjusting the Shortest Bar setting affects the proportion of bars to one another

To edit a conditional formatting rule after you've applied it:

1 From the Conditional Formatting menu, choose Manage Rules to open the Conditional Formatting Rules Manager dialog box.

2 Double-click the rule you want to edit to open the Edit Formatting Rule dialog box.

3 Select settings as needed. For example, to make data bars more accurately reflect their proportion to one another, select Number from the Type list under Shortest Bar, and then type 0 (zero) in the Value box.

4 Click OK in each dialog box.

Do it!

A-1: Creating data bars

Here's how	Here's why
1 Open Graphics	From the current unit folder.
Activate the Sales Per Quarter sheet	(If necessary.) You'll create data bars to graphically depict the values in the Total sales column.
2 Save the workbook as **My graphics**	In the current unit folder.
3 Select G5:G19	
4 Activate the Home tab	If necessary.
5 In the Styles group, click **Conditional Formatting**	To display the Conditional Formatting menu.
6 Choose the first item in the Data Bars submenu, as indicated	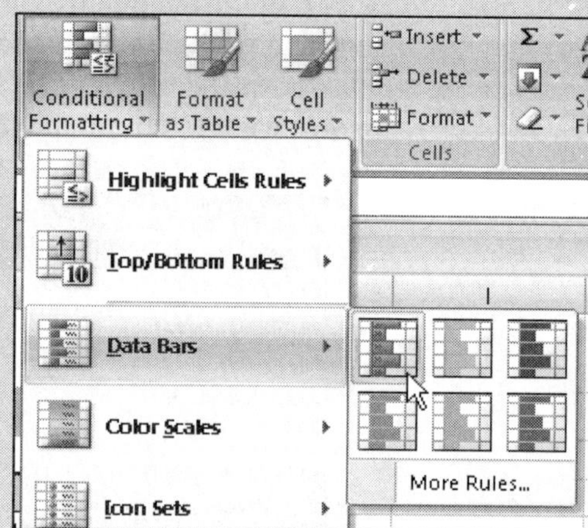 To create blue data bars in the selected cells.
Click outside the selected range	To deselect the range containing the data bars. The bars show up better when the cells are deselected.
Widen column G to 20	To make the data bars longer. The bars now appear as shown in Exhibit 8-1. You'll change the data bars so they represent a range from zero to the largest value, rather than having the shortest bar based on the smallest value.

7	In the Styles group, from the Conditional Formatting menu, choose **Manage Rules...**	To open the Conditional Formatting Rules Manager. Because the default setting displays rules for only the current selection, no rules appear yet.
	From the "Show formatting rules for" list, select **This Worksheet**	To display the Data Bar rule you created.
	Double-click **Data Bar**	To open the Edit Formatting Rule dialog box.
8	From the Type list under Shortest Bar, select **Number**	To base the shortest bar's length on a fixed value.
9	Verify that 0 appears in the Value box under Shortest Bar	
	Click **OK**	To close the Edit Formatting Rule dialog box.
	Click **OK**	To close the Conditional Formatting Rules Manager dialog box. The data bars now appear as shown in Exhibit 8-2. The bar for the smallest value ($6,700) is approximately half the length of the bar for the largest value ($16,840), so the bars are in proportion to the values. However, there is less contrast between the bar lengths. There are valid reasons to use different approaches (basing the shortest bar on the smallest value or on a fixed value) for different purposes.
10	Update the workbook	

Color scales

Explanation

Like data bars, color scales are used to format cells depending on their values. Color scales are applied based on a continuum of colors that correspond to the cell's values. This continuum can be based on shades of one color; for instance, the lowest values can be a dark green while the highest values show a light green. You can also show a transition between two or three colors, such as reds for lower values, yellows for middle values, and greens for higher values.

		Sales per quarter				
Salesperson	Rating	Qtr1	Qtr2	Qtr3	Qtr4	Total sales
Bill MacArthur		$1,500	$1,750	$1,500	$2,700	$7,450
Jamie Morrison		$3,560	$3,000	$1,700	$2,000	$10,260
Maureen O'Connor		$4,500	$4,000	$3,500	$3,700	$15,700
Rebecca Austin		$3,250	$2,725	$3,000	$3,250	$12,225
Paul Anderson		$2,520	$2,500	$2,500	$2,700	$10,220
Cynthia Roberts		$1,500	$1,700	$1,800	$2,000	$7,000
Rita Greg		$4,590	$4,050	$4,500	$3,700	$16,840
Trevor Johnson		$3,660	$3,200	$3,000	$2,250	$12,110
Kevin Meyers		$1,790	$1,800	$2,000	$2,200	$7,790
Adam Long		$1,700	$1,950	$2,500	$2,750	$8,900
Kendra James		$1,650	$2,000	$1,500	$1,750	$6,900
Michael Lee		$2,050	$2,500	$2,800	$3,200	$10,550
Sandra Lawrence		$3,425	$3,750	$4,000	$3,120	$14,295
Mary Smith		$4,540	$2,700	$3,000	$3,200	$13,440
Annie Philips		$1,200	$1,700	$1,800	$2,000	$6,700

Exhibit 8-3: Cells under Qtr1 are conditionally formatted with color scales

Do it!

A-2: Using color scales

Here's how	Here's why
1 Select C5:C19	You'll conditionally format this range with color scales.
2 Display the Conditional Formatting menu	
From the Color Scales submenu, choose the indicated option	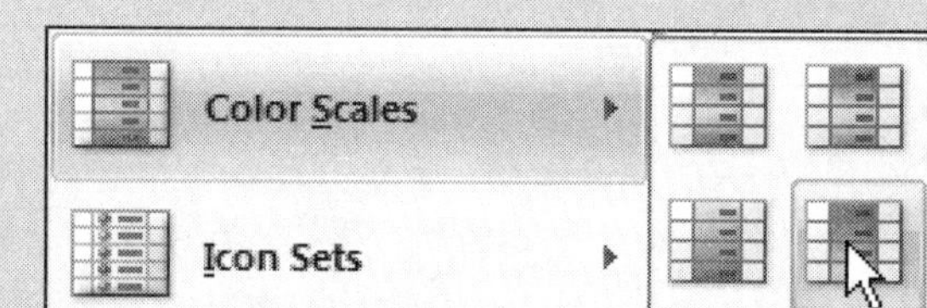 The second option in the second row.
Deselect the range	The cells are formatted from yellow to red, with shades of red representing the higher values.
3 Update the workbook	

Icon sets

Explanation

You can also use conditional formatting to divide values graphically into groups. For example, you can assign a green, yellow, or red dot to represent good, fair, or poor values. To create this effect, apply *icon set* conditional formatting, as shown in Exhibit 8-4.

Sales per quarter						
Salesperson	Rating	Qtr1	Qtr2	Qtr3	Qtr4	Total sales
Bill MacArthur	○	$1,500	$1,750	$1,500	$2,700	$7,450
Jamie Morrison	◑	$3,560	$3,000	$1,700	$2,000	$10,260
Maureen O'Connor	●	$4,500	$4,000	$3,500	$3,700	$15,700
Rebecca Austin	◑	$3,250	$2,725	$3,000	$3,250	$12,225
Paul Anderson	◔	$2,520	$2,000	$2,500	$2,700	$9,720
Cynthia Roberts	○	$1,500	$1,700	$1,800	$2,000	$7,000
Rita Greg	●	$4,590	$4,050	$4,500	$3,700	$16,840
Trevor Johnson	◑	$3,660	$3,200	$3,000	$2,250	$12,110
Kevin Meyers	◔	$1,790	$1,800	$2,000	$2,200	$7,790
Adam Long	◔	$1,700	$1,950	$2,500	$2,750	$8,900
Kendra James	○	$1,650	$2,000	$1,500	$1,750	$6,900
Michael Lee	◑	$2,050	$2,500	$2,800	$3,200	$10,550
Sandra Lawrence	◕	$3,425	$3,750	$4,000	$3,120	$14,295
Mary Smith	◕	$4,540	$2,700	$3,000	$3,200	$13,440
Annie Philips	○	$1,200	$1,700	$1,800	$2,000	$6,700

Exhibit 8-4: The Rating column with icon sets applied, representing five ratings

You apply and edit icon set formatting much as you would data bars. Here are some options you might consider changing:

- Displaying only the icons and not the values. (If desired, you can paste-link the values into another column so the values appear in a separate column from the icons.)
- Choosing fixed values for the cutoffs for each icon. By default, icon set formatting assigns a value range of the same size to each icon. If each icon should represent a specific sales or rating goal, for example, you can specify that instead.

Do it!

A-3: Creating icon sets

Here's how	Here's why
1 Select B5	In column B, you'll create icon sets representing ratings for the salespeople based on their total sales. For you to do this, column B must contain the same values as the Total sales column.
2 Type **=**	To begin the formula.
Click G5 and press ENTER	To complete the formula.
Copy the formula down the column	Excel fills the result down the entire column, duplicating the values from the Total sales column.
3 Select B5:B19	
Display the Conditional Formatting menu and choose **Icon Sets**	To open the Icon Sets gallery.
In the Icon Sets gallery, select the indicated option	
	An icon appears on the left side of each cell, along with the cell's value. In this set, the solid black circle represents the highest values, and the outlined circle represents the lowest values.
	You'll edit the rule that affects this column's formatting.
4 From the Conditional Formatting menu, choose **Manage Rules**	To open the Conditional Formatting Rules Manager.
Double-click **Icon Set**	To open the Edit Formatting Rule dialog box.
Under Edit the Rule Description, check **Show Icon Only**	(In the bottom-right corner of the dialog box.) To hide the values in this column.
	You'll also change the "breakpoints" (the threshold values) that determine which icon is displayed for a given value.
5 From each list under Type, select **Number**	To base each icon on a specific range of numeric values.

6	In the Value box to the right of the top icon, enter **15000**	(The solid black circle.) To specify that only sales of $15,000 or greater receive the icon representing the Excellent rating.
	In the Value box to the right of the second icon, enter **12500**	(The circle that's three-quarters black.) To specify that only sales between $12,500 and $15,000 receive the icon representing the Good rating.
	In the Value box to the right of the third icon, enter **10000**	The half-black circle indicates sales between $10,000 and $12,500. These numbers are considered "Fair" and meet the sales goal.
	In the last Value box, enter **7500**	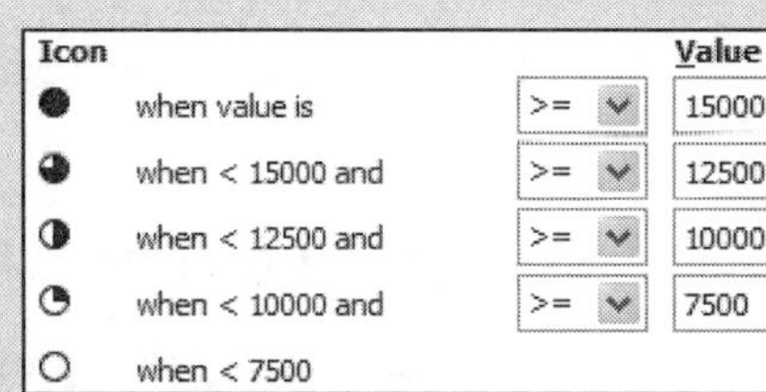 Sales between $7,500 and $10,000 are short of the goal, and sales below $7,500 are considered "Poor."
7	Click **OK**	To close the Edit Formatting Rule dialog box.
	Click **OK**	To close the Conditional Formatting Rules Manager dialog box.
	Center-align the icon column	The ratings appear as shown in Exhibit 8-4. Conditional formatting is dynamic, so changing sales values may change the icon displayed.
8	In D9, enter **2500**	This brings Paul Anderson's total sales to over $10,000, earning him a fair rating.
9	Update the workbook	

Topic B: SmartArt graphics

This topic covers the following Microsoft Certified Application Specialist exam objective for Excel 2007.

#	Objective
4.4.2	**Insert and modify SmartArt graphics**
	• Insert SmartArt graphics
	• Modify SmartArt graphics using Quick Styles
	• Add effects to SmartArt graphics

Inserting SmartArt graphics

Explanation

A SmartArt graphic provides a visual representation of information. Excel 2007 provides many SmartArt graphic layouts that you can use to create objects to communicate your messages or ideas by combining shapes and text. After you've created an object, you can change the graphic's layout, content, and formatting.

To insert a SmartArt graphic, do this:

1. On the Insert tab, in the Illustrations group, click SmartArt.
2. Select a format.
3. Click OK.

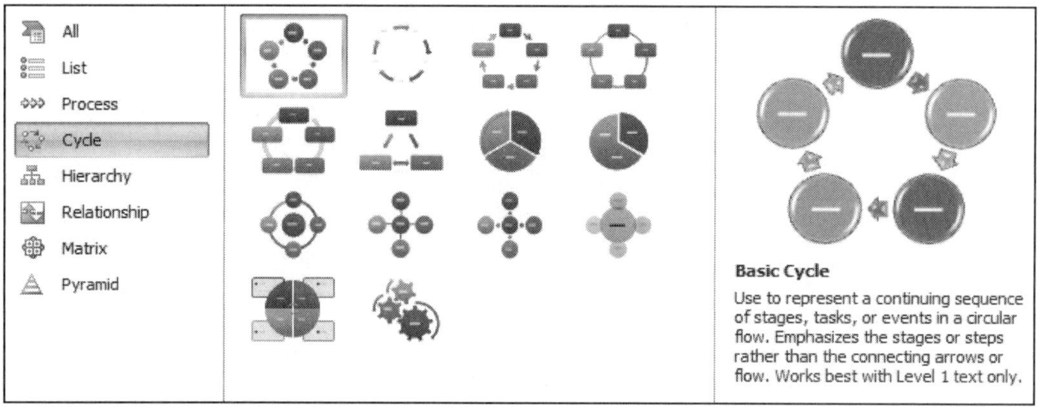

Exhibit 8-5: You can choose from many formats for SmartArt graphics

After you insert the graphic, you can change its layout, format, colors, text, and just about any other property. You can also apply 3D effects, so objects can look tilted, contoured, or textured.

When you insert or work with SmartArt graphics, Excel displays the SmartArt Tools, adding Design and Format tabs to the Ribbon.

Do it!

B-1: Inserting a SmartArt graphic

Here's how	Here's why
1 Activate the SmartArt sheet	It's blank.
2 On the Insert tab, in the Illustrations group, click **SmartArt**	To open the Choose a SmartArt Graphic dialog box.
3 In the left pane, select **Cycle**	
In the center pane, select the first format	(Basic Cycle.) A description appears on the right side.
4 Click **OK**	The basic cycle diagram appears on the sheet with default colors and effects. You'll change these next.
5 Update the workbook	

Modifying SmartArt

Explanation

After inserting a SmartArt graphic, you can set about customizing it as you choose. First, select the graphic (click it). Then, you can use the tools and Quick Style buttons on the SmartArt Tools | Design and Format tabs.

Quick Style buttons apply several formatting properties at once, but you can also adjust all these properties individually. You can customize the overall look of the graphic, the individual shapes, and the text.

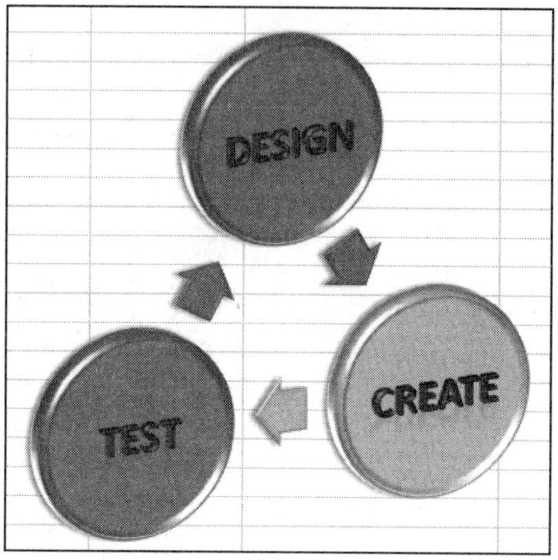

Exhibit 8-6: SmartArt with 3D effects and WordArt applied

Do it!

B-2: Modifying a SmartArt graphic

Here's how	Here's why
1 Select the SmartArt graphic	(If necessary.) You'll change some of its properties.
2 Activate the SmartArt Tools | Format tab	
Observe the tools	The Shape Styles and WordArt Styles groups offer both "Quick Style" buttons and tools for tweaking each item's properties individually.
3 Activate the SmartArt Tools | Design tab	There are also many options here to format the graphic.
4 If you have room, drag the corners or edges of the SmartArt graphic frame outward	You can see the effects better if the shapes and text are bigger.
5 Click one of the shapes, but don't select the text	Click inside the shape but outside the [Text] area.
Press DELETE	To delete the shape.

6	Delete another shape	(Select any one and press Delete.) You should be left with three shapes.
7	In the top shape, click **[Text]**	To edit the text in the shape.
	Enter **Design**	You'll make a simple cycle diagram.
8	In the lower-right circle, enter **Create** as the text	Click [Text] and type "Create."
9	In the lower-left circle, enter **Test**	You now have a simple blue diagram.
	Deselect the shape	Click inside the graphic's frame but outside the shapes.
10	In the SmartArt Styles group, click **Change Colors** and choose the indicated option	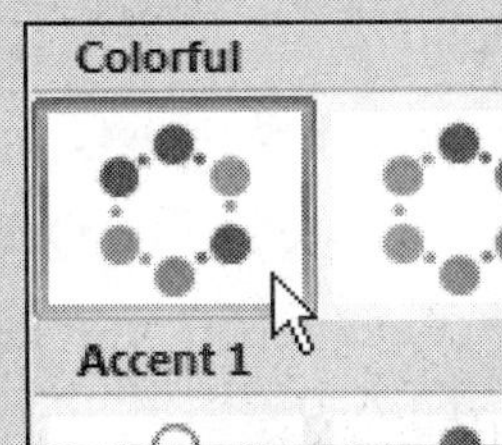
11	On the right side of the SmartArt Styles group, click the More button, as shown	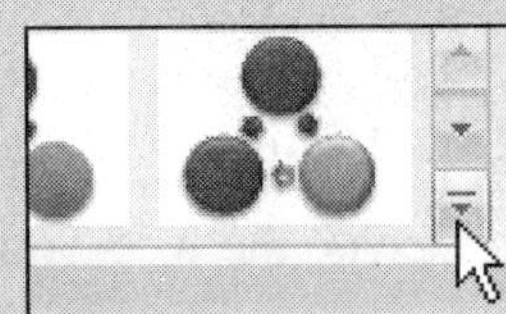
		To display some available 3D effects.
	Choose a 3D effect	(Any one will do.) Note that as you mouse over an effect, you can see a preview of it applied to your graphic.
12	Activate the SmartArt Tools | Format tab	
	In the WordArt Styles group, select a Quick Style for the text that contrasts well with the shape style you chose	Click the More button to the right of the Quick Styles and choose a style. Note that as you mouse over a style, you can see a preview of it applied to your graphic.
13	In the WordArt Styles group, click **Text Effects** and choose **3-D Rotation**	
	Select a rotation	Your graphic might now look something like Exhibit 8-6.
14	Update and close the workbook	

Unit summary: Conditional formatting and SmartArt

Topic A

In this topic, you expressed data graphically within cells by applying three forms of **conditional formatting**: data bars, color scales, and icon sets.

Topic B

In this topic, you learned how to insert a **SmartArt** graphic. Then you learned how to modify that graphic by using the tools on the SmartArt Tools | Design and Format tabs, which include **Quick Styles** and other options.

Independent practice activity

In this activity, you'll create data bars and icon sets, and create and modify a SmartArt graphic.

1 Open **Practice Graphics**. Save the workbook as **My practice graphics**.

2 Activate the 4th Quarter Sales sheet, if necessary.

3 Conditionally format the Qtr4 column with data bars. To do so, select C5:C19. Then, on the Home tab, click Conditional Formatting, choose Data Bars, and choose any color.

4 Add an icon set to the Rating column. (*Hint*: Set the column values equal to the Qtr4 values. After adding the icon set, set the column to show only the icons.)

5 Update the workbook.

6 Activate the Art Practice sheet.

7 Add a SmartArt graphic showing a hierarchy chart.

8 Fill in just a few names and positions of a fictitious company. Add and remove shapes as necessary.

9 Format the chart with effects and colors of your choosing.

10 Update and close the workbook.

11 Close Excel.

Review questions

1 What's the difference between data bars and color scales?

2 How can you make data bars look more proportional to one another?

3 True or false? You can choose shades of only one or two colors for color scale formatting.

4 What are Quick Styles in the context of SmartArt graphics?

Course summary

This summary contains information to help you bring the course to a successful conclusion. Using this information, you will be able to:

A Use the summary text to reinforce what you've learned in class.

B Determine the next courses in this series (if any), as well as any other resources that might help you continue to learn about Excel 2007.

Topic A: Course summary

Use the following summary text to reinforce what you've learned in class.

Unit summaries

Unit 1

In this unit, you learned how to use the **IF** and **SUMIF** functions to evaluate data on the basis of specified criteria. Then, you learned how to round off a number by using the **ROUND** function. Finally, you learned how to use the **PMT** function to calculate the periodic payment for a loan.

Unit 2

In this unit, you learned how to use **lookup functions** to find a specific value in a worksheet. You learned how to use VLOOKUP to search for a value in a list that is arranged vertically. Next, you learned how to use the **MATCH** function to find the relative position of a value in a range. You also learned how to use the **INDEX** function to find a value in a range by specifying row and column numbers. Finally, you learned how to create **one-variable** and **two-variable data tables** to project values.

Unit 3

In this unit, you learned how to **validate data** entered in cells. Then, you learned how to use **database functions** to summarize values that meet complex criteria.

Unit 4

In this unit, you learned how to create and add fields to a **PivotTable**. Next, you learned how to display different views of data by moving fields and by hiding and showing details in the PivotTable. Then, you learned how to **format** PivotTable data by applying a style and changing field settings. Finally, you learned how to create **PivotCharts** to graphically display data from the PivotTable.

Unit 5

In this unit, you learned how to **export data** from Excel to a text file. You also learned how to **import data** from a text file into an Excel workbook. Next, you learned how to import and export **XML data** by using the XML Source task pane. Finally, you learned how to use **Microsoft Query** to retrieve data from an Access database. You also learned how to use the **Web query** feature to get data from a Web page.

Unit 6

In this unit, you learned how to use **Goal Seek** and **Solver** to meet a target output for a formula by adjusting the values of input cells. Next, you learned how to install and use the **Analysis ToolPak**. Then, you learned how to create **scenarios** to save various sets of values in a worksheet. Finally, you learned how to create **views** to save different sets of worksheet display and print settings.

Unit 7

In this unit, you learned how to run a **macro** that automatically performed tasks for you. You also learned how to record a macro, as well as how to assign a macro to a button so that users can run the macro by clicking the button. Next, you learned how to **edit the VBA code** for a macro. Finally, you learned how to create **custom functions**.

Unit 8

In this unit, you learned how to represent data graphically within cells by applying three forms of **conditional formatting**: data bars, color scales, and icon sets. You also learned how to insert **SmartArt** graphics and how to modify them by using **Quick Styles** and other options.

Topic B: Continued learning after class

It is impossible to learn to use any software effectively in a single day. To get the most out of this class, you should begin working with Excel 2007 to perform real tasks as soon as possible. We also offer resources for continued learning.

Next courses in this series

This is the third course in this series. The next courses in this series are:

- *Excel 2007: Power User*
- *Excel 2007: VBA Programming*

Other resources

For more information, visit www.axzopress.com.

Excel 2007: Advanced

Quick reference

Button	Shortcut keys	Function
		Collapses a dialog box.
		Expands a dialog box.
	CTRL + Z	Undoes the last step.
	CTRL + C	Copies the contents of a cell.
	CTRL + V	Pastes the copied contents into a cell.
	ALT + =	Automatically sums values in an adjacent range of cells.
		Hides details in a PivotTable or outline.
		Shows details in a PivotTable or outline.
	ALT + F5	Updates a PivotTable with the latest data.
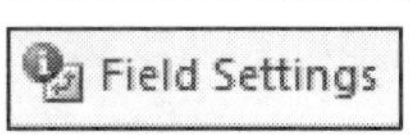	ALT + L	Opens the PivotTable Field dialog box.
		Inserts a PivotChart based on data in a worksheet's PivotTable.
		Opens the New Web Query dialog box.
	ALT + F8	Opens the Macro dialog box.

Button	Function
	Begins the process of recording a macro.
	Stops recording a macro.
	Opens the Data Validation dialog box.
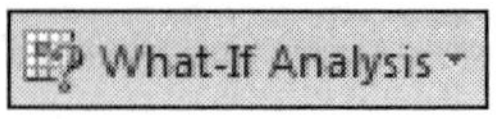	Displays a menu of data analysis tools.

Glossary

Arguments
The values that a function uses for calculations.

Color scales
A type of conditional formatting that applies colors to cells, based on the cells' values.

Comments
Non-executable lines of text used to describe sections of macro code.

Data bars
Bars that are displayed within cells to represent their values relative to other cells in a range.

Data table
A range that displays the results of changing certain values in one or more formulas.

Database
An organized collection of related information.

Field
A column of data in a database. Also, a category of data in a PivotTable.

Function procedure
A procedure containing the code which, when executed, performs a sequence of steps and then returns a value.

Goal Seek utility
A tool used to solve a formula based on the value that you want the formula to return.

HLOOKUP
A horizontal lookup function used to find values in a table that has column labels.

Icon set
A type of conditional formatting in which you use a group of icons to represent ranges of values.

Input cell
The location where various values are substituted from a data table.

Macro
A series of instructions that are executed automatically with a single command.

Microsoft Query
A program used to retrieve data that meets certain conditions in one or more tables of a database.

Modules
The special sheets in which VBA code is stored.

Name
A meaningful description that you assign to a cell or range.

Nested function
A function that serves as an argument of another function.

PivotTable
An interactive table that summarizes, organizes, and compares large amounts of data in a worksheet.

Record
A row of data in a database.

Return value
The result of a function procedure.

Scenario
A set of input values that produce different results.

Solver utility
A tool used to perform complex what-if analysis by adjusting the values in multiple cells used in a formula.

Source data
The data on which a PivotTable is based.

Sub procedure
A procedure containing the code which, when executed, performs a sequence of steps.

VBA (Visual Basic for Applications)
The code, or language, in which Excel saves the steps of a macro.

Views
Different sets of worksheet display and print settings that you can save.

VLOOKUP
A vertical lookup function used to find values in a table that has row labels.

What-if analysis
The process of changing the values in a worksheet and observing how these changes affect the results of formulas.

XML (Extensible Markup Language)
A set of rules for structuring and designing data formats that are exchanged between applications.

Index

A

Analysis ToolPak
  Installing, 6-5
  Tools in, 6-11
AND function, 1-4
AVERAGE function, 1-12
AVERAGEIFS function, 1-13

C

Color scales, 8-6
Conditional formatting, 8-2
COUNTIF function, 1-11
COUNTIFS function, 1-13

D

Data
  Analyzing, 6-2
  Exporting as text file, 5-2
  Exporting to XML files, 5-16
  Importing text files, 5-4
  Importing XML data, 5-15
  Refreshing in PivotTables, 4-11
  Retrieving from Web pages, 5-23
  Sampling, 6-12
  Validating, 3-2, 3-5
Data bars, 8-2
Data tables
  Defined, 2-12
  One-variable, 2-12
  Two-variable, 2-14
Database functions, 3-8
Database, defined, 3-8
DAVERAGE function, 3-11
DCOUNT function, 3-8
DSUM function, 3-8, 3-11

E

Evaluation order of conditions in functions, 1-16

F

Fields
  Adding to PivotTables, 4-5
  Changing settings of, 4-14
  Moving in PivotTables, 4-7
  Types of, 4-2
Files, saving with macros, 7-6
Formulas, hiding and showing, 1-21
Function procedures, 7-14
Functions
  AND, OR, and NOT, 1-4
  AVERAGE, 1-12
  AVERAGEIFS, 1-13
  COUNTIF, 1-11
  COUNTIFS, 1-13
  Custom, 7-14
  DAVERAGE, 3-8, 3-11
  DCOUNT, 3-8
  DSUM, 3-8, 3-11
  Evaluation order for conditions in, 1-16
  HLOOKUP, 2-2, 2-6, 2-7
  IF, 1-2
  IFERROR, 1-8
  INDEX, 2-10
  MATCH, 2-8
  Nesting, 1-4
  PMT, 1-19
  ROUND, 1-16
  SUMIF, 1-9
  SUMIFS, 1-13
  VLOOKUP, 2-2, 2-4, 2-5

G

Goal Seek utility, 6-2
Graphics, SmartArt, 8-10

H

HLOOKUP function, 2-2, 2-6, 2-7

I

Icon sets, 8-7
IF function, 1-2
  Nesting, 1-7
IFERROR function, 1-8
INDEX function, 2-10

M

Macros
  Assigning to buttons, 7-9
  Editing, 7-12
  Enabling, 7-3
  Recording, 7-6
  Running, 7-2
  Saving, 7-6
MATCH function, 2-8
Microsoft Query, 5-18

N

Nested functions, 1-4
NOT function, 1-4

O

OR function, 1-4

P

PivotCharts, creating, 4-16
PivotTables
  Adding fields to, 4-5
  Changing field settings for, 4-14
  Collapsing and expanding details, 4-9
  Creating, 4-3
  Defined, 4-2
  Formatting, 4-12
  Rearranging, 4-7
  Refreshing data in, 4-11
PMT function, 1-19

Q

Querying external databases
  With Microsoft Query, 5-18
  With Web query, 5-22

R

Records, removing duplicates of, 5-8
Report Filter fields, 4-2
ROUND function, 1-16

S

Sampling analysis tool, 6-12
Scenarios
  Creating, 6-14
  Creating a summary report, 6-20
  Merging, 6-20
  Switching among, 6-17
SmartArt graphics, 8-10
Solver utility, 6-2
  Installing, 6-5
  Using, 6-7
Source data, 4-2
Sub procedures, 7-10
SUMIF function, 1-9
SUMIFS function, 1-13

T

Text files, importing, 5-4
Text, converting to columns, 5-7
Trust Center, 7-3

V

VBA code
  Editing, 7-12
  Modules, 7-10
  Statements vs. comments, 7-10
Views
  Creating, 6-22
  Switching among, 6-24
VLOOKUP function, 2-2, 2-4, 2-5

W

Web queries, 5-22
What-if analysis, 6-2
Workbooks
  Mapping to XML schema, 5-10
  Setting macro security levels for, 7-3

X

XML
  Defined, 5-10
  Exporting data in XML format, 5-16
  Importing XML data, 5-15
  Vs. HTML, 5-22
XML maps
  Creating, 5-10
  Deleting, 5-17
XML Source task pane, 5-10